GRAPHIC LIBRARY™

INVENTIONS AND DISCOVERY

ISAAC NEWTON AND THE

LAWS of MOTION

by Andrea Gianopoulos
illustrated by Phil Miller and
Charles Barnett III

Capstone

Mankato, Minnesota

Graphic Library is published by Capstone Press,
151 Good Counsel Drive, P.O. Box 669, Mankato, Minnesota 56002.
www.capstonepress.com

Printed in the United States of America

1 2 3 4 5 6 12 11 10 09 08 07

Library of Congress Cataloging-in-Publication Data
Gianopoulos, Andrea.
Isaac Newton and the laws of motion / by Andrea Gianopoulos; illustrated by Phil Miller and Charles Barnett III.
p. cm.—(Graphic library. Inventions and discovery)
Includes bibliographical references and index.
ISBN-13: 978-0-7368-6847-1 (hardcover)
ISBN-10: 0-7368-6847-X (hardcover)
ISBN-13: 978-0-7368-7899-9 (softcover pbk.)
ISBN-10: 0-7368-7899-8 (softcover pbk.)
1. Newton, Isaac, Sir, 1642–1727—Juvenile literature. 2. Motion—Juvenile literature. 3. Physicists—Great Britain—Biography—Juvenile literature. I. Title. II. Series.
QC16.N7G53 2007
530.092—dc22 2006026909
[B]

Summary: In graphic novel format, tells the story of how Isaac Newton developed the laws of motion and the law of universal gravitation.

Designer
Alison Thiele

Production Designer
Kyle Grenz

Colorist
Otha Zackariah Edward Lohse

Editor
Tom Adamson

Capstone Press thanks Paul Zitzewitz, Professor of Physics and Science Education at the University of Michigan-Dearborn, for his help in preparing this book.

Editor's note: Direct quotations from primary sources are indicated by a yellow background.

Direct quotations appear on the following pages:
Pages 13, 26, quoted in *Never at Rest: A Biography of Isaac Newton* by Richard S. Westfall (Cambridge University Press, 1980).
Page 13 (paper), from *The Principia* by Isaac Newton, as quoted in *On the Shoulders of Giants: The Great Works of Physics and Astronomy*, edited by Stephen Hawking (Philadelphia: Running Press, 2002).

TABLE OF

CONTENTS

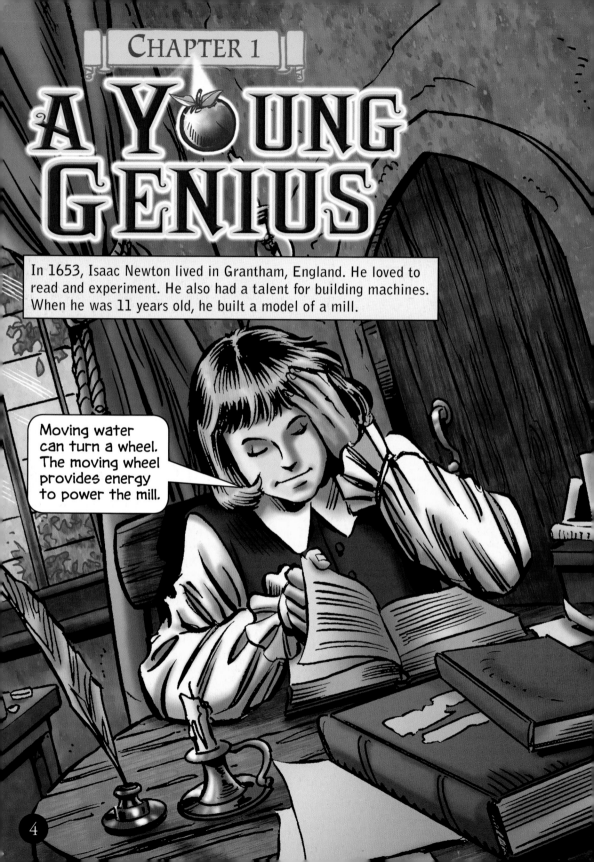

CHAPTER 1

A YOUNG GENIUS

In 1653, Isaac Newton lived in Grantham, England. He loved to read and experiment. He also had a talent for building machines. When he was 11 years old, he built a model of a mill.

Moving water can turn a wheel. The moving wheel provides energy to power the mill.

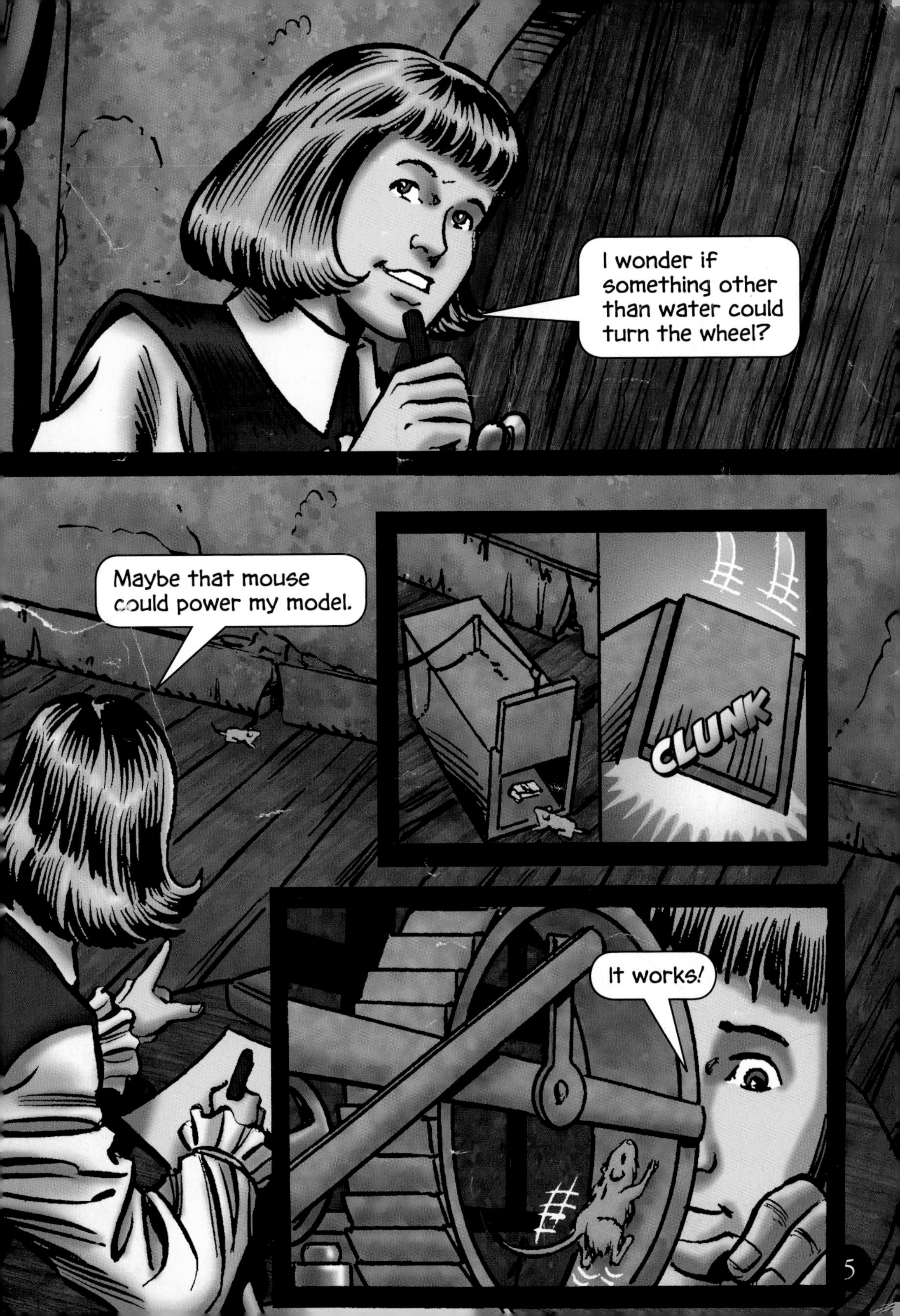
I wonder if something other than water could turn the wheel?
Maybe that mouse could power my model.
CLUNK
It works!

While he went to grammar school, Newton lived with someone his family knew in Grantham. Mr. Clark and his family owned the apothecary, or drugstore there. The chemical powders, liquids, and crystals in the store fascinated young Newton.

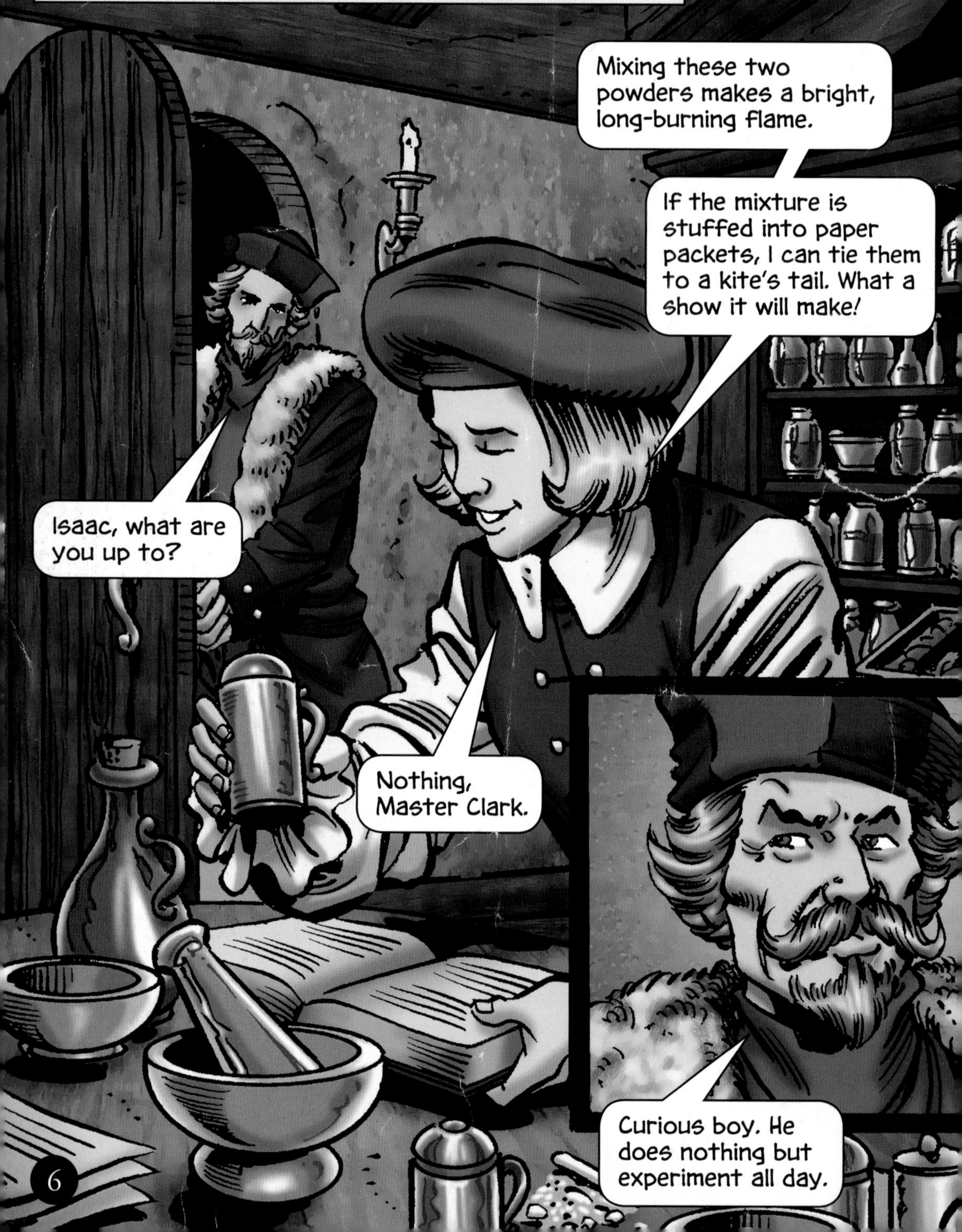
Mixing these two powders makes a bright, long-burning flame.
If the mixture is stuffed into paper packets, I can tie them to a kite's tail. What a show it will make!
Isaac, what are you up to?
Nothing, Master Clark.
Curious boy. He does nothing but experiment all day.

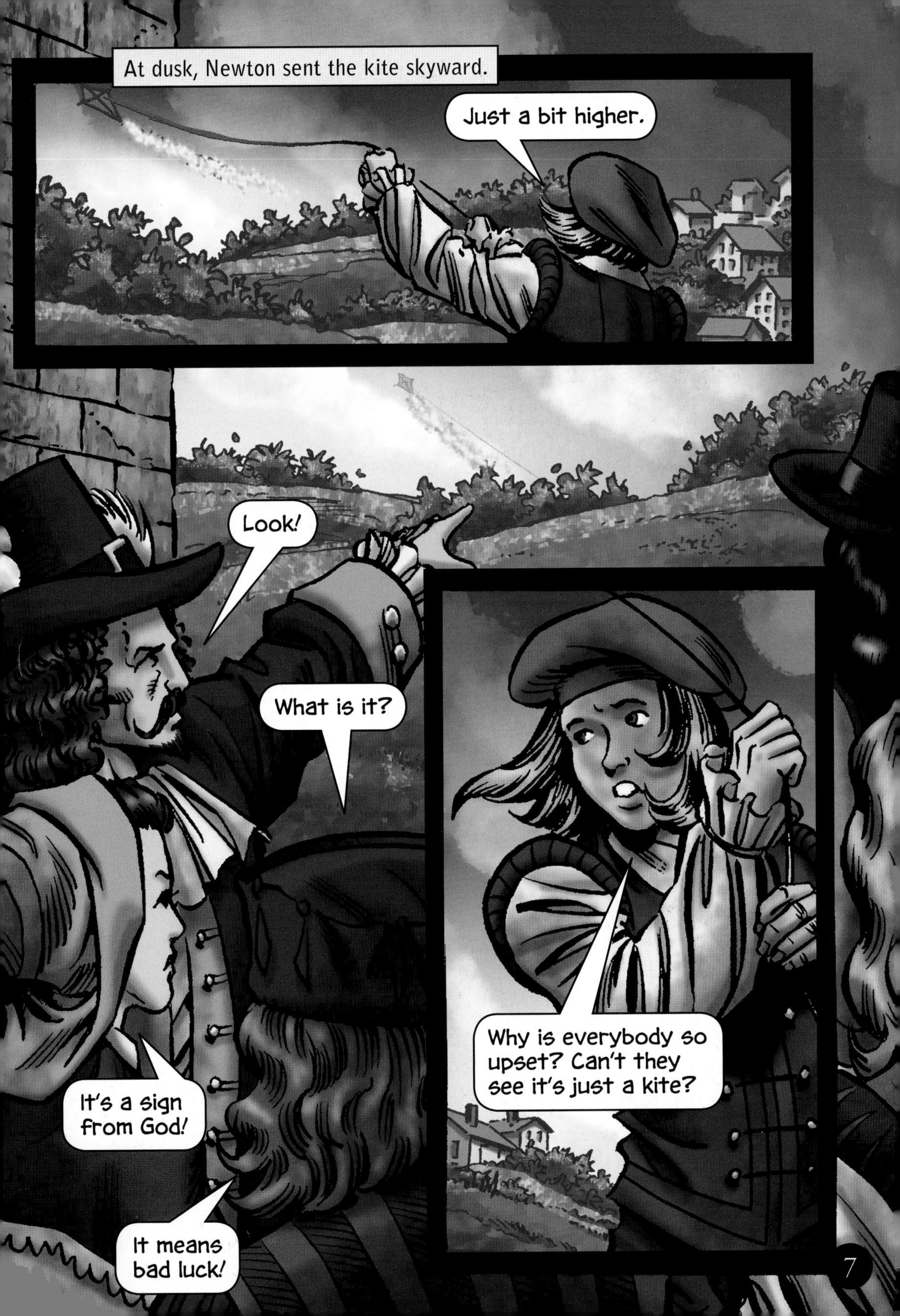
At dusk, Newton sent the kite skyward.
Just a bit higher.
Look!
What is it?
It's a sign from God!
It means bad luck!
Why is everybody so upset? Can't they see it's just a kite?

Chapter 2

Birth of a Masterpiece

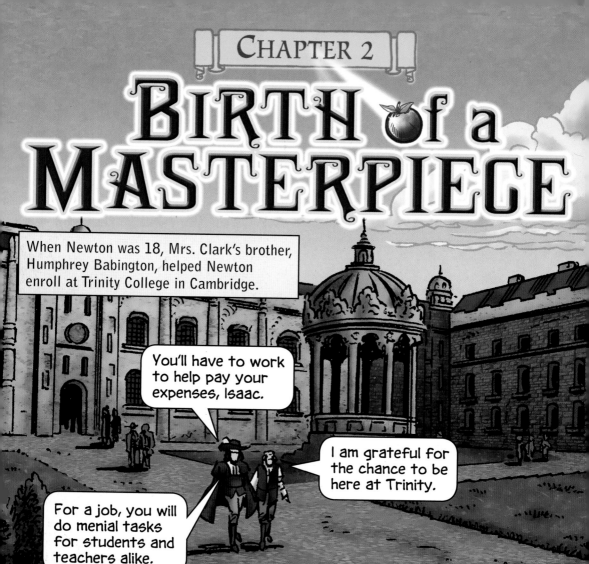

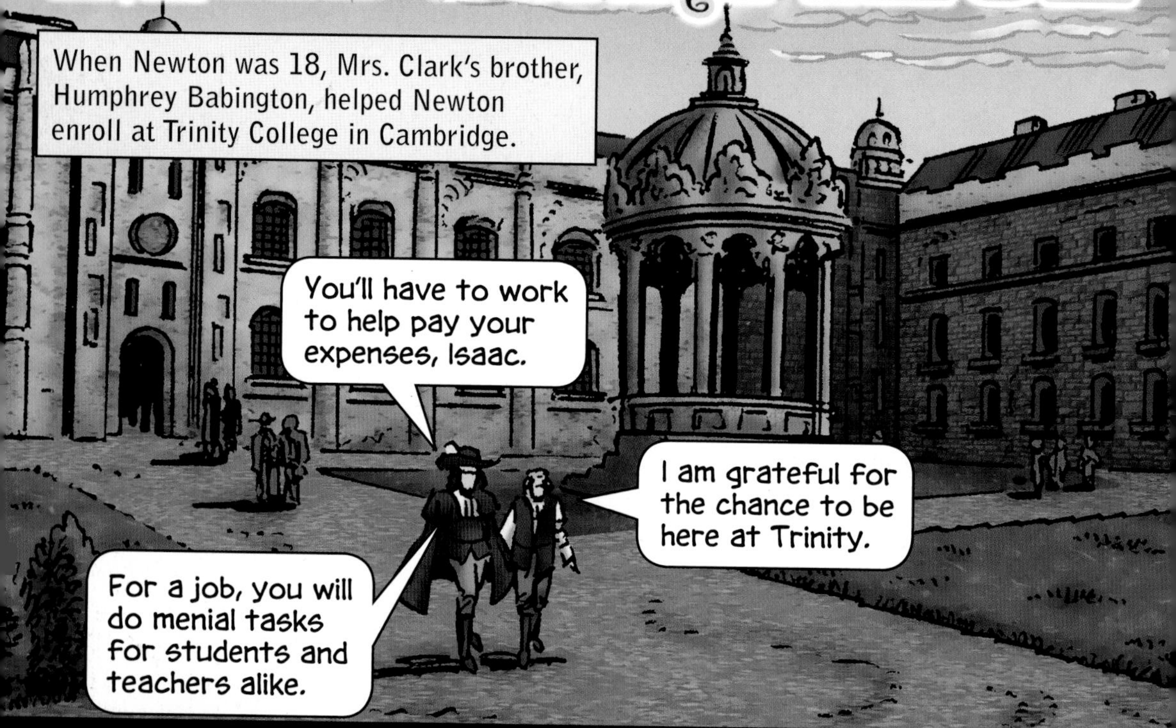
When Newton was 18, Mrs. Clark's brother, Humphrey Babington, helped Newton enroll at Trinity College in Cambridge.
You'll have to work to help pay your expenses, Isaac.
I am grateful for the chance to be here at Trinity.
For a job, you will do menial tasks for students and teachers alike.

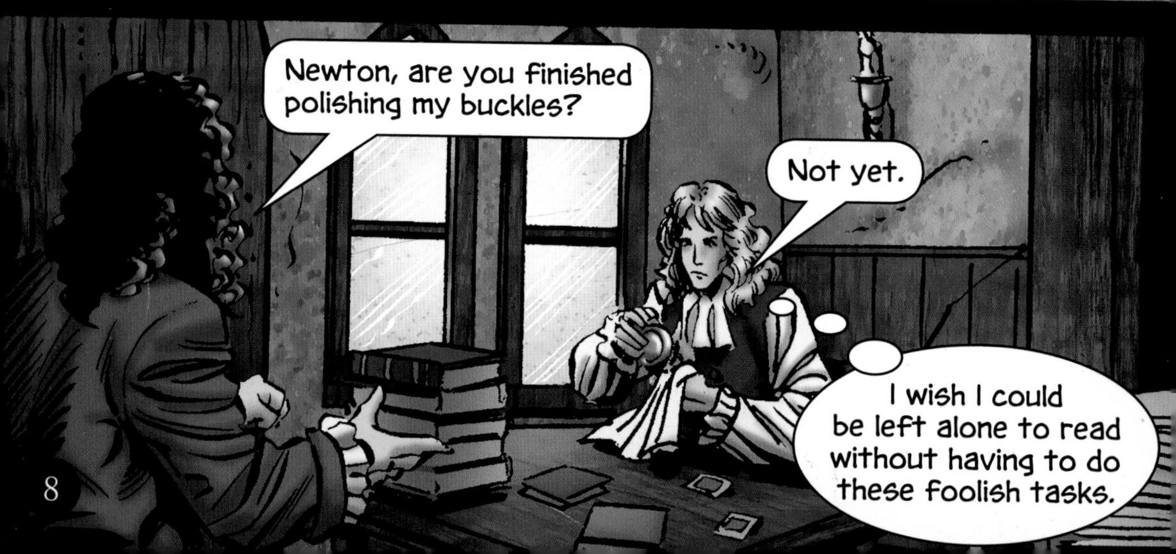
Newton, are you finished polishing my buckles?
Not yet.
I wish I could be left alone to read without having to do these foolish tasks.

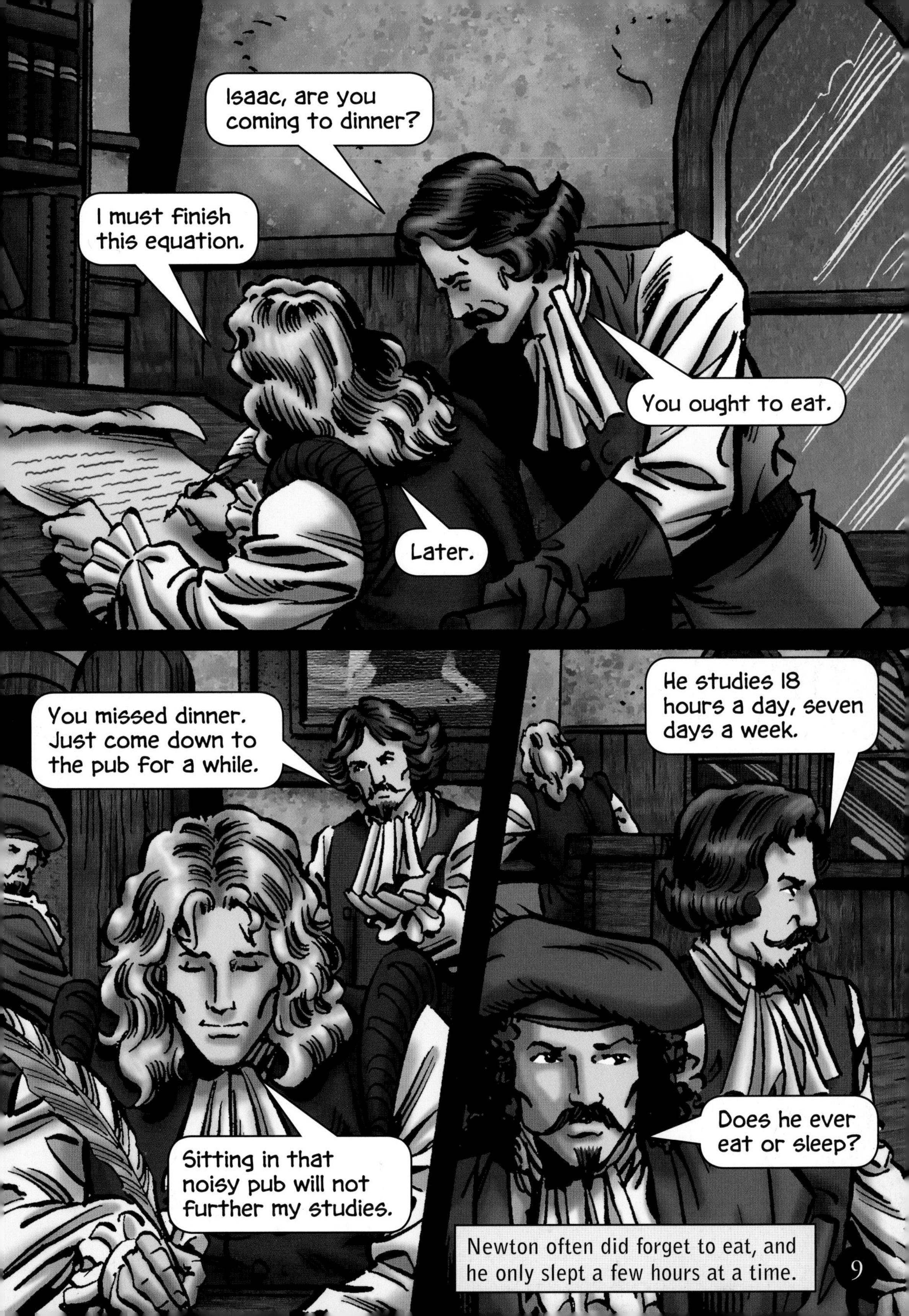
Isaac, are you coming to dinner?
I must finish this equation.
You ought to eat.
Later.
You missed dinner. Just come down to the pub for a while.
Sitting in that noisy pub will not further my studies.
He studies 18 hours a day, seven days a week.
Does he ever eat or sleep?
Newton often did forget to eat, and he only slept a few hours at a time.

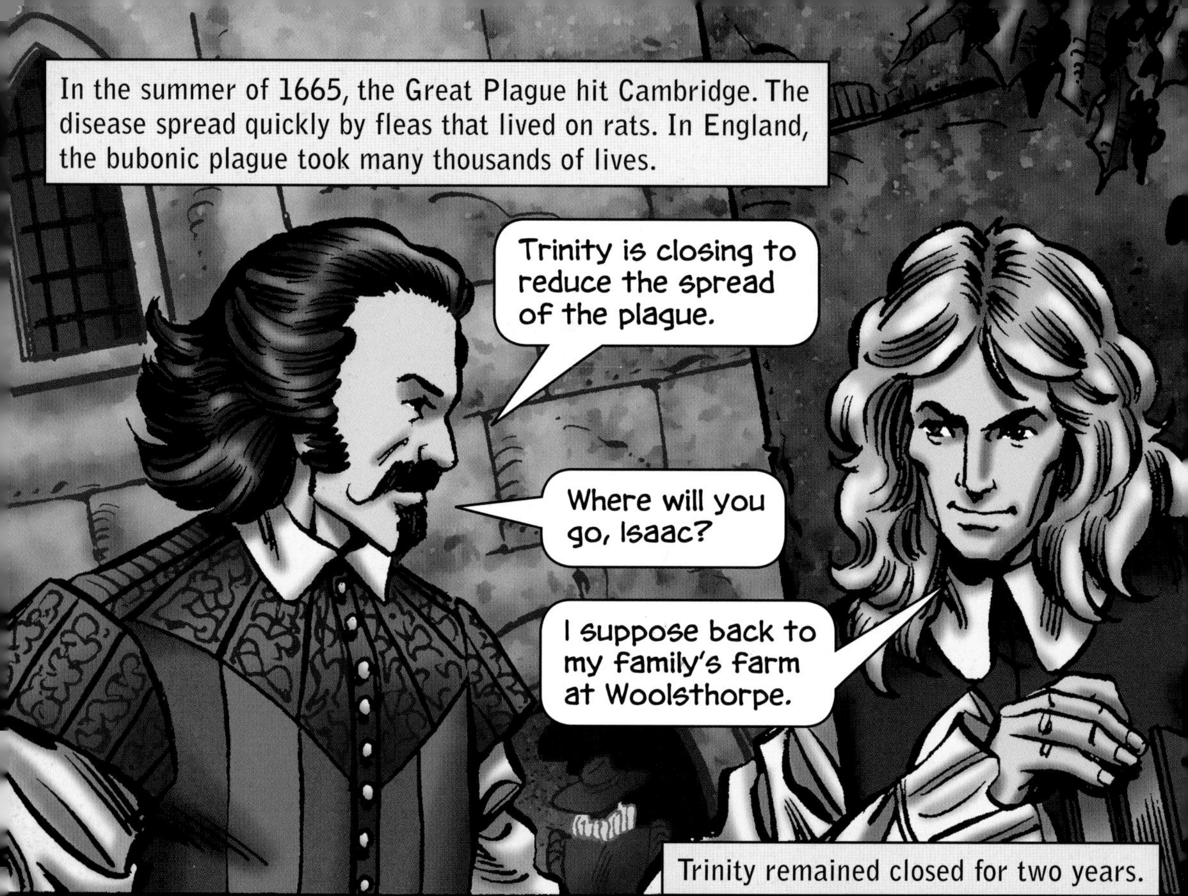
In the summer of 1665, the Great Plague hit Cambridge. The disease spread quickly by fleas that lived on rats. In England, the bubonic plague took many thousands of lives.
Trinity is closing to reduce the spread of the plague.
Where will you go, Isaac?
I suppose back to my family's farm at Woolsthorpe.
Trinity remained closed for two years.

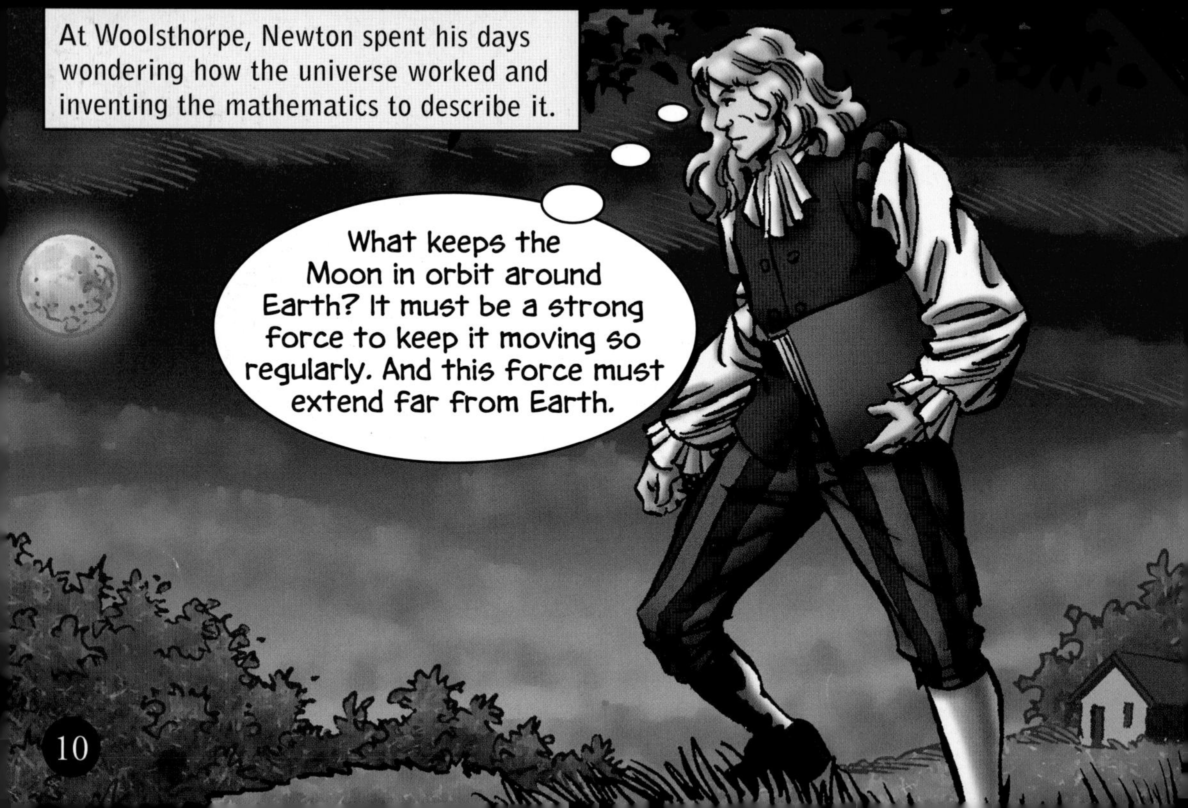
At Woolsthorpe, Newton spent his days wondering how the universe worked and inventing the mathematics to describe it.
What keeps the Moon in orbit around Earth? It must be a strong force to keep it moving so regularly. And this force must extend far from Earth.

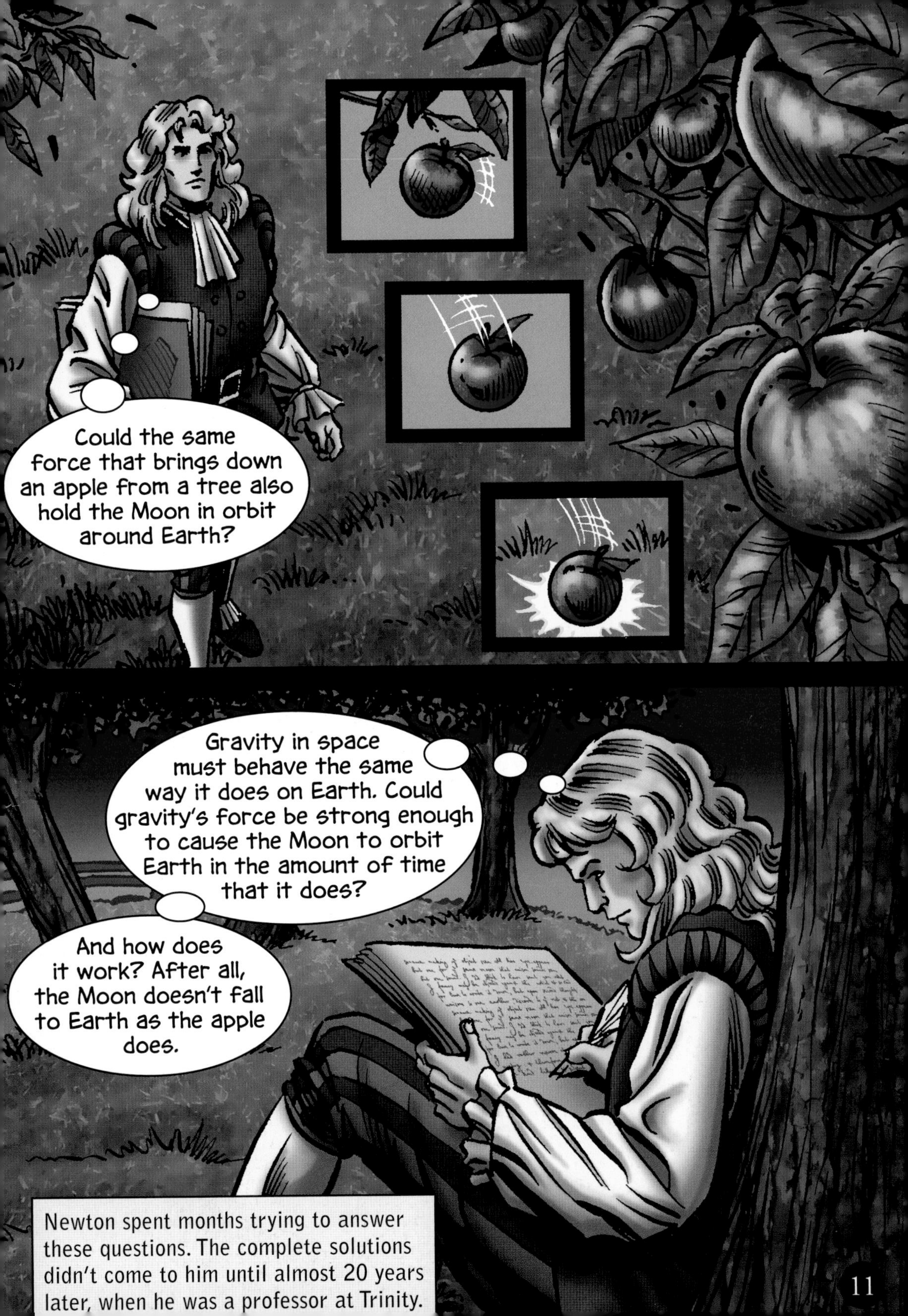
Could the same force that brings down an apple from a tree also hold the Moon in orbit around Earth?
Gravity in space must behave the same way it does on Earth. Could gravity's force be strong enough to cause the Moon to orbit Earth in the amount of time that it does?
And how does it work? After all, the Moon doesn't fall to Earth as the apple does.
Newton spent months trying to answer these questions. The complete solutions didn't come to him until almost 20 years later, when he was a professor at Trinity.

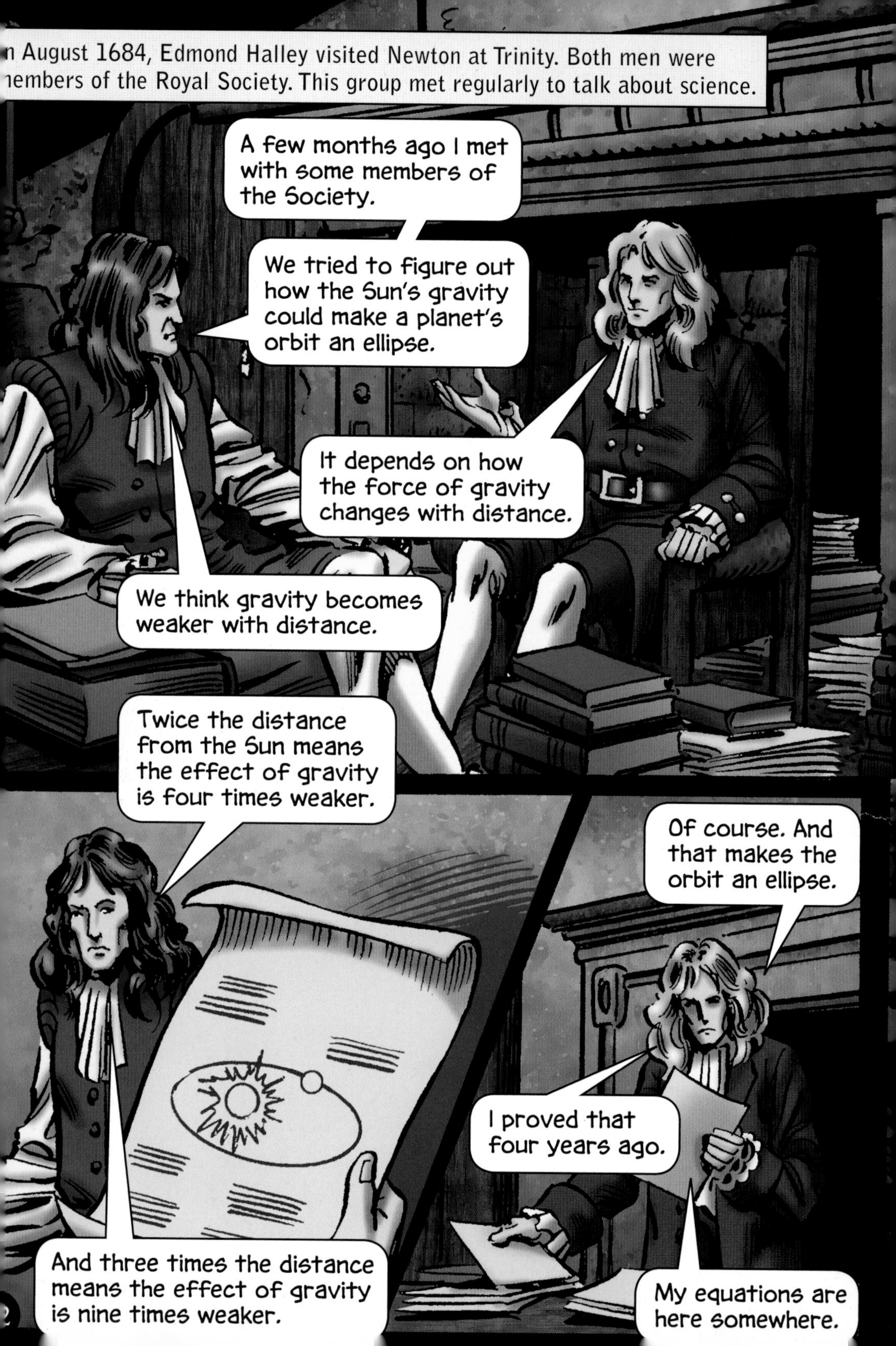

n August 1684, Edmond Halley visited Newton at Trinity. Both men were embers of the Royal Society. This group met regularly to talk about science.
A few months ago I met with some members of the Society.
We tried to figure out how the Sun's gravity could make a planet's orbit an ellipse.
It depends on how the force of gravity changes with distance.
We think gravity becomes weaker with distance.
Twice the distance from the Sun means the effect of gravity is four times weaker.
And three times the distance means the effect of gravity is nine times weaker.
Of course. And that makes the orbit an ellipse.
I proved that four years ago.
My equations are here somewhere.

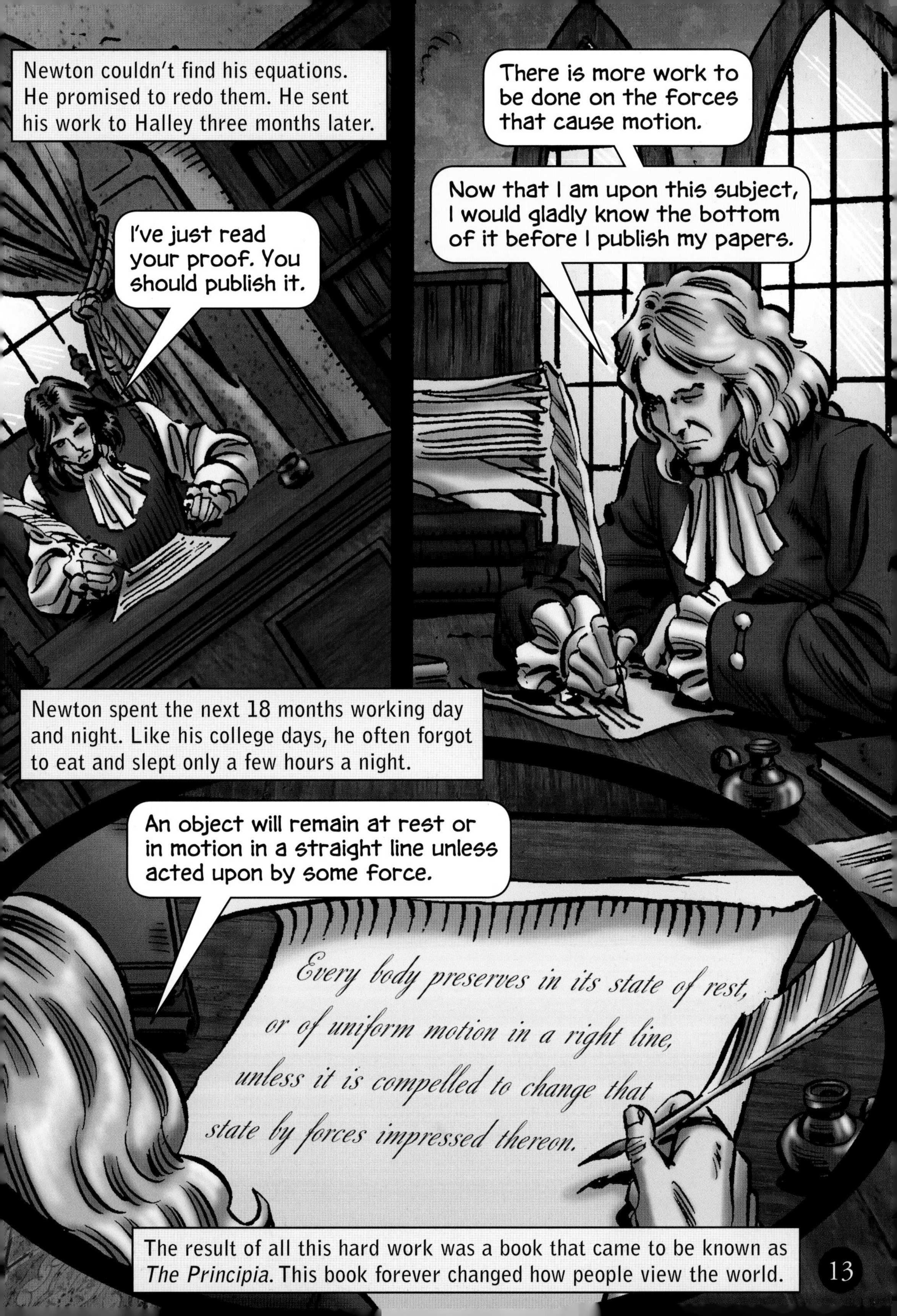

Newton couldn't find his equations. He promised to redo them. He sent his work to Halley three months later.
I've just read your proof. You should publish it.
There is more work to be done on the forces that cause motion.
Now that I am upon this subject, I would gladly know the bottom of it before I publish my papers.
Newton spent the next 18 months working day and night. Like his college days, he often forgot to eat and slept only a few hours a night.
An object will remain at rest or in motion in a straight line unless acted upon by some force.
Every body preserves in its state of rest, or of uniform motion in a right line, unless it is compelled to change that state by forces impressed thereon.
The result of all this hard work was a book that came to be known as *The Principia*. This book forever changed how people view the world.

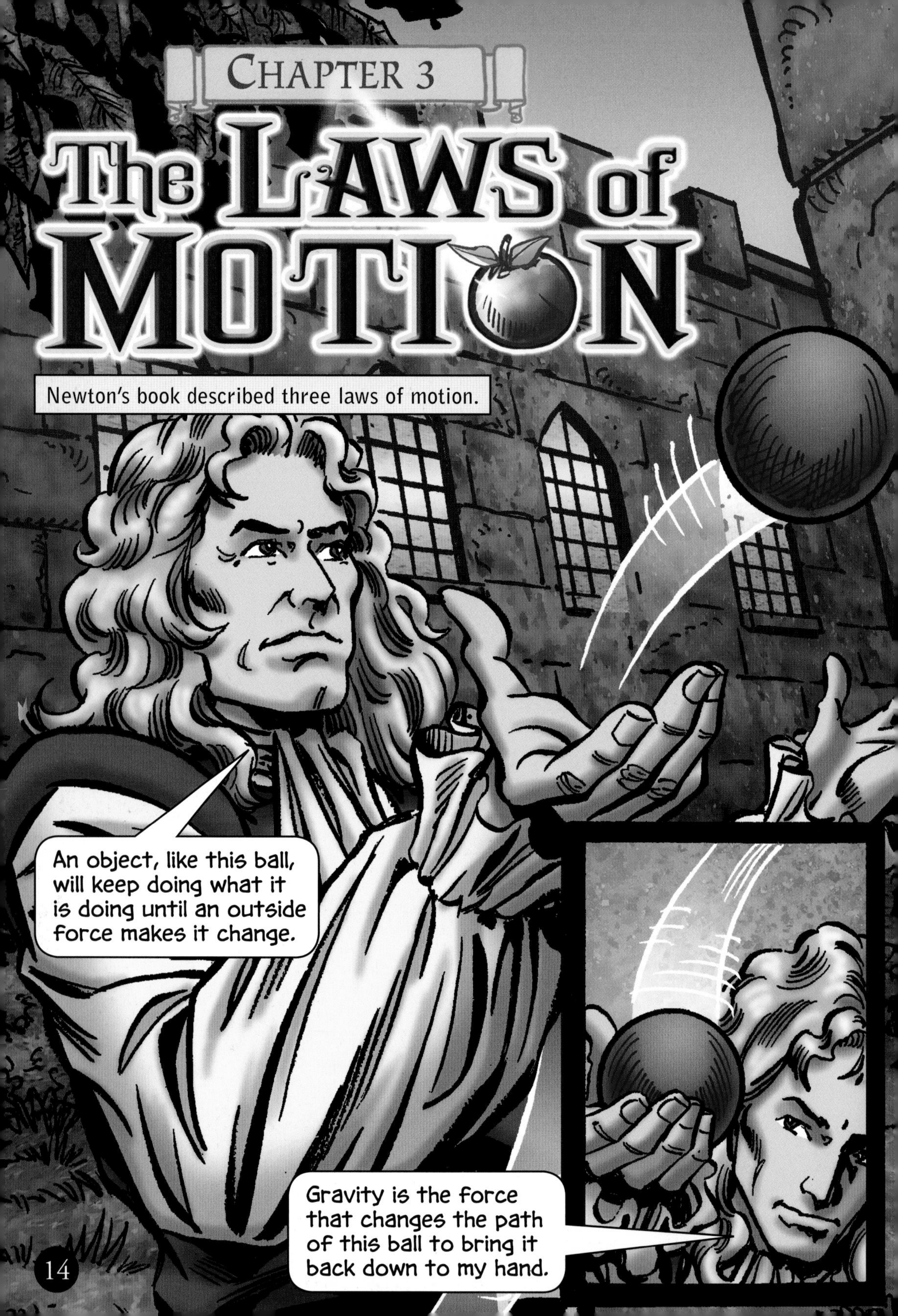

CHAPTER 3
The LAWS of MOTION
Newton's book described three laws of motion.
An object, like this ball, will keep doing what it is doing until an outside force makes it change.
Gravity is the force that changes the path of this ball to bring it back down to my hand.

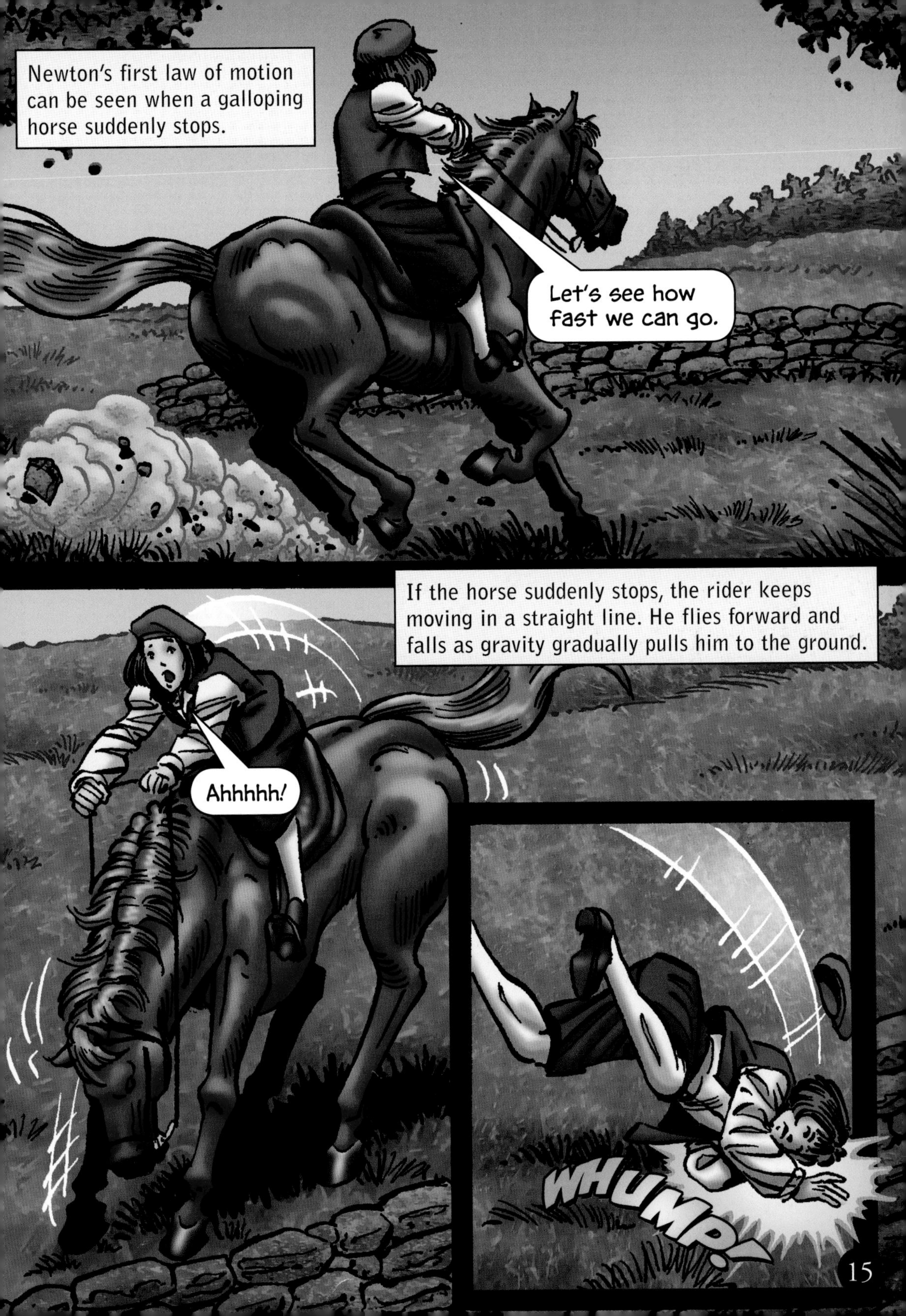
Newton's first law of motion can be seen when a galloping horse suddenly stops.
Let's see how fast we can go.
If the horse suddenly stops, the rider keeps moving in a straight line. He flies forward and falls as gravity gradually pulls him to the ground.
Ahhhhh!
WHUMP!

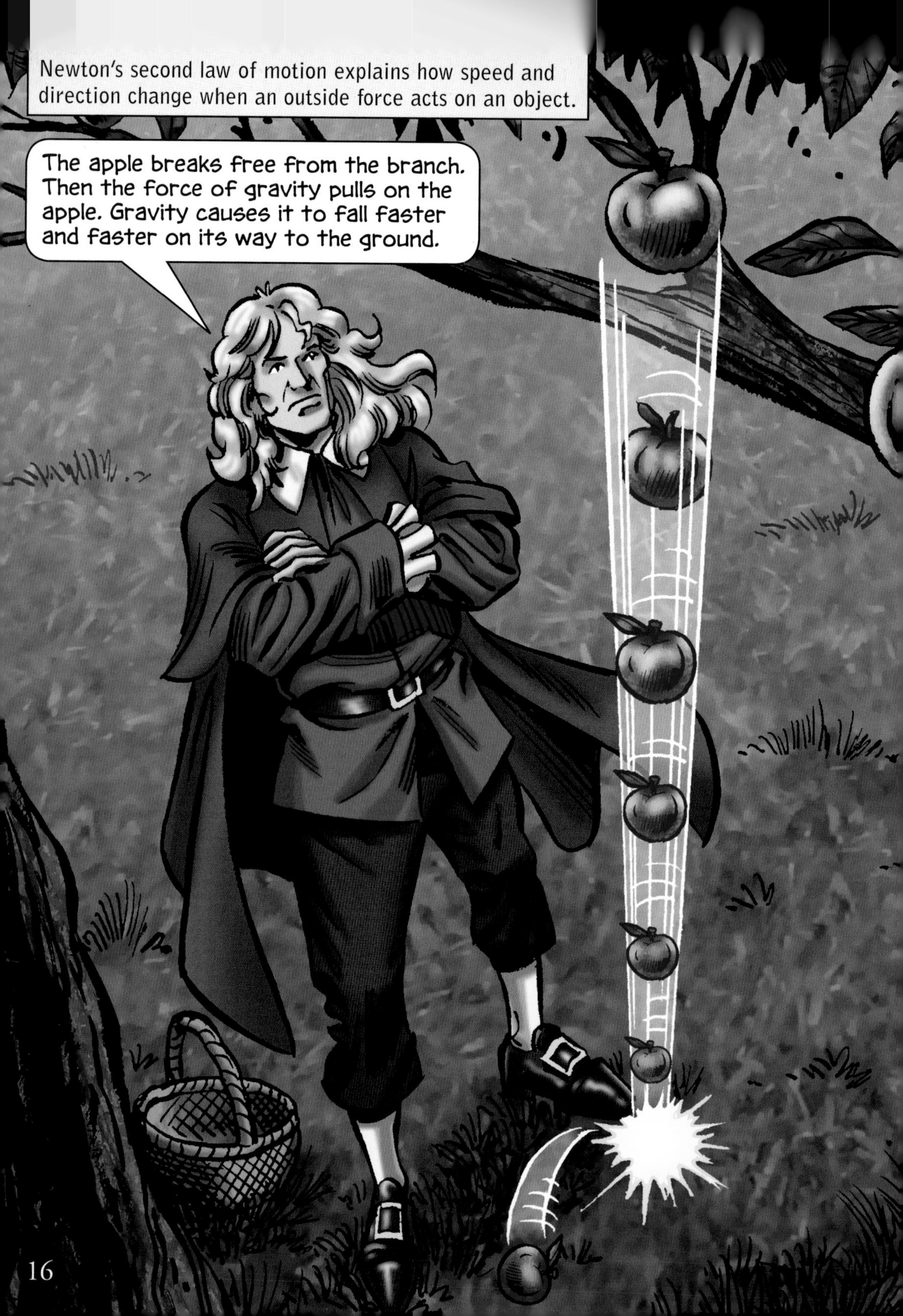
Newton's second law of motion explains how speed and direction change when an outside force acts on an object.
The apple breaks free from the branch. Then the force of gravity pulls on the apple. Gravity causes it to fall faster and faster on its way to the ground.

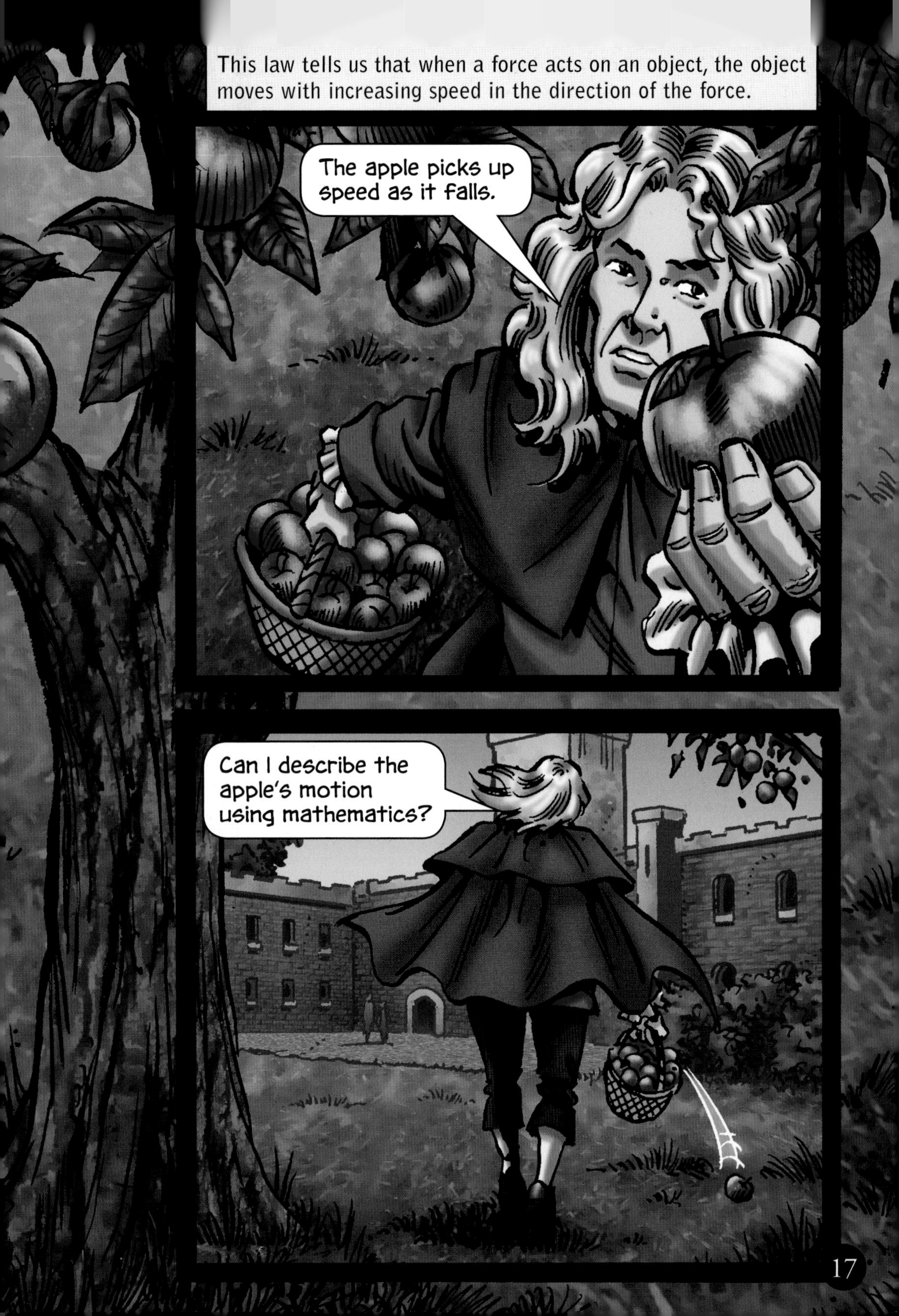
This law tells us that when a force acts on an object, the object moves with increasing speed in the direction of the force.
The apple picks up speed as it falls.
Can I describe the apple's motion using mathematics?

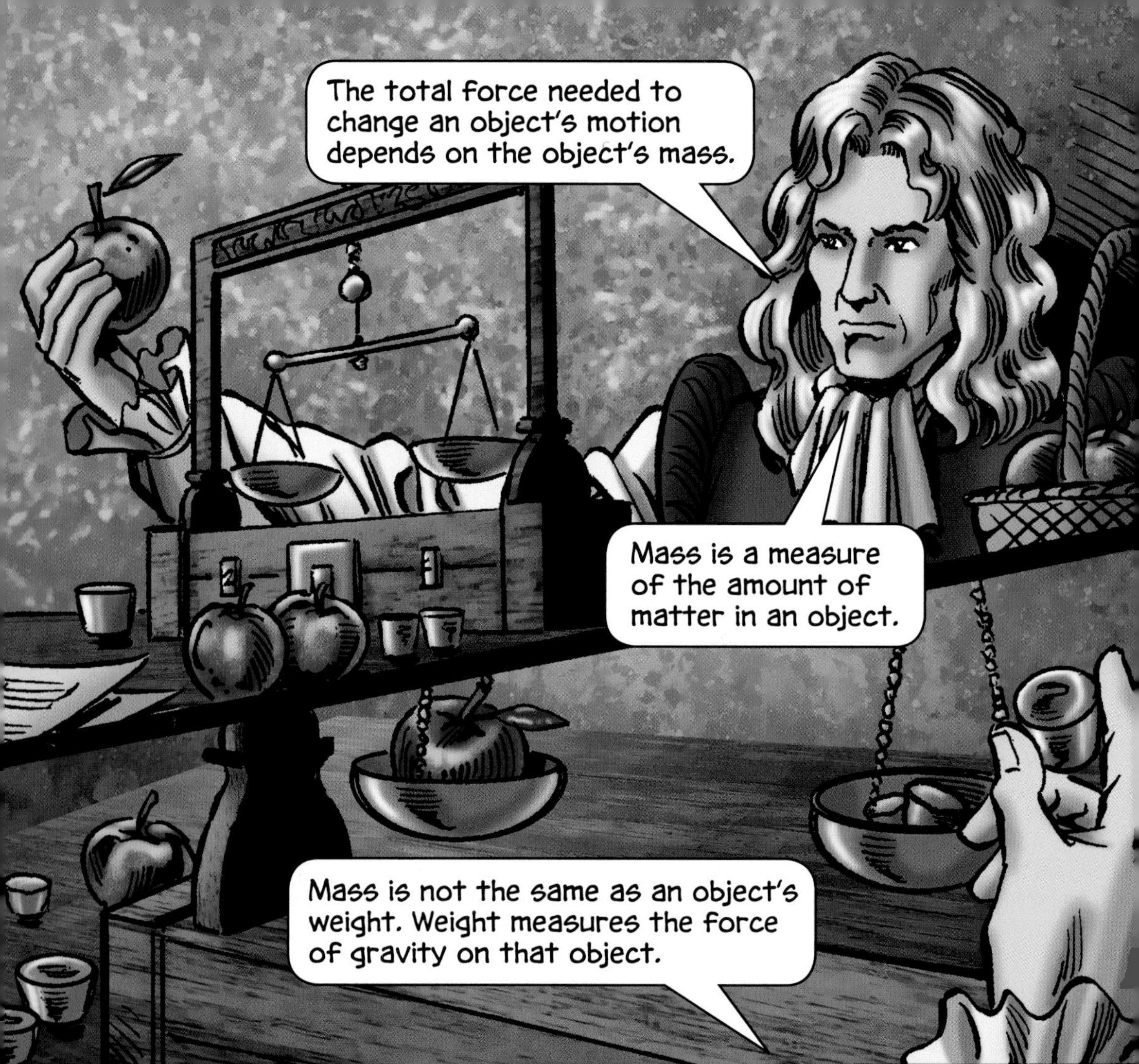
The total force needed to change an object's motion depends on the object's mass.
Mass is a measure of the amount of matter in an object.
Mass is not the same as an object's weight. Weight measures the force of gravity on that object.

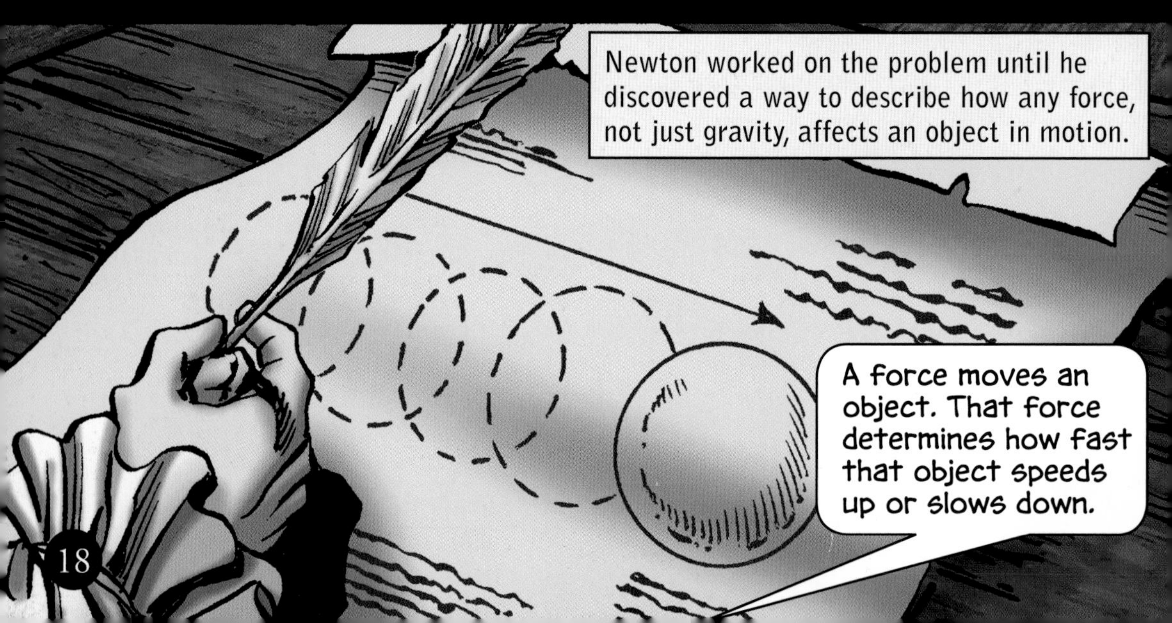
Newton worked on the problem until he discovered a way to describe how any force, not just gravity, affects an object in motion.
A force moves an object. That force determines how fast that object speeds up or slows down.

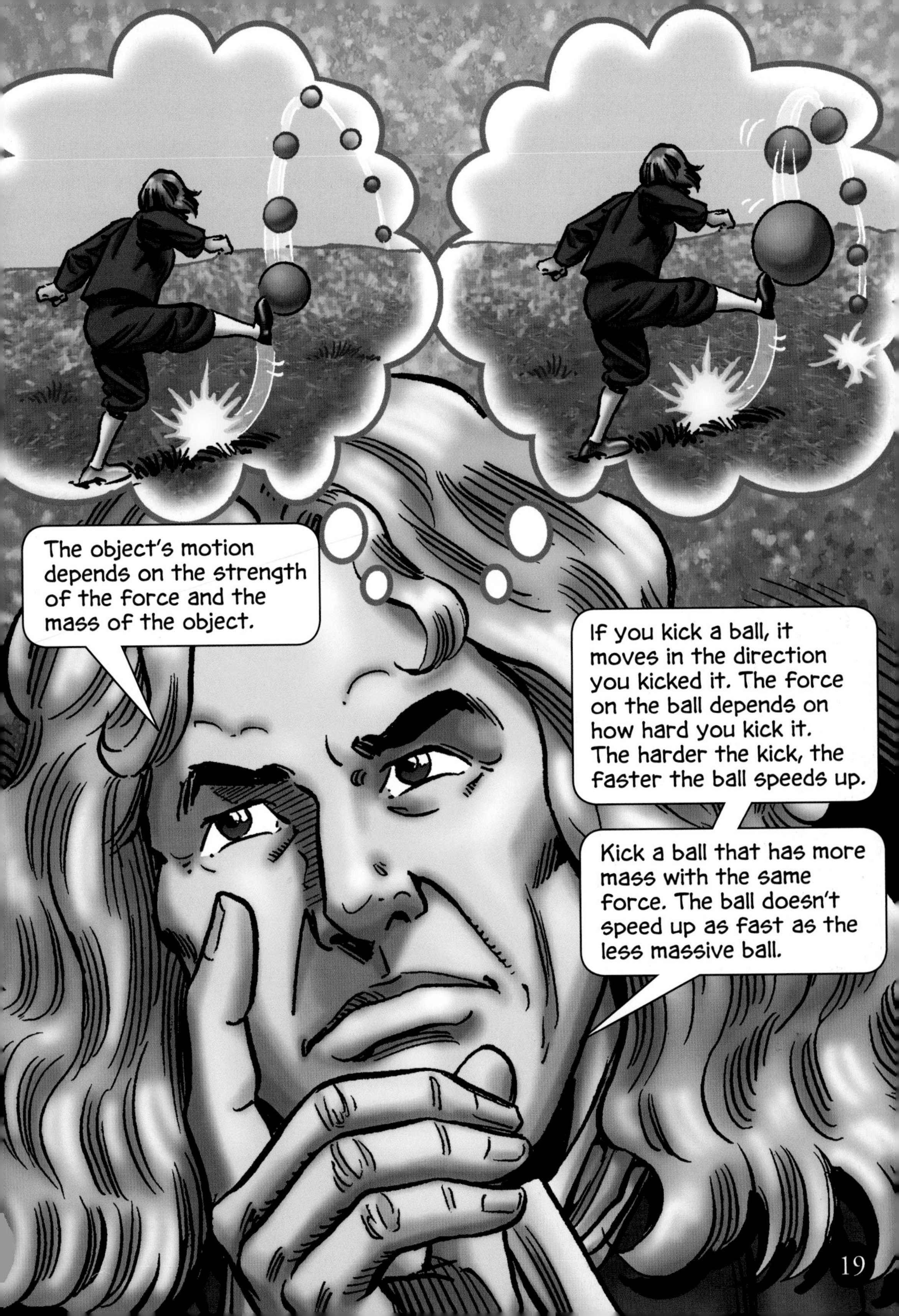
The object's motion depends on the strength of the force and the mass of the object.
If you kick a ball, it moves in the direction you kicked it. The force on the ball depends on how hard you kick it. The harder the kick, the faster the ball speeds up.
Kick a ball that has more mass with the same force. The ball doesn't speed up as fast as the less massive ball.

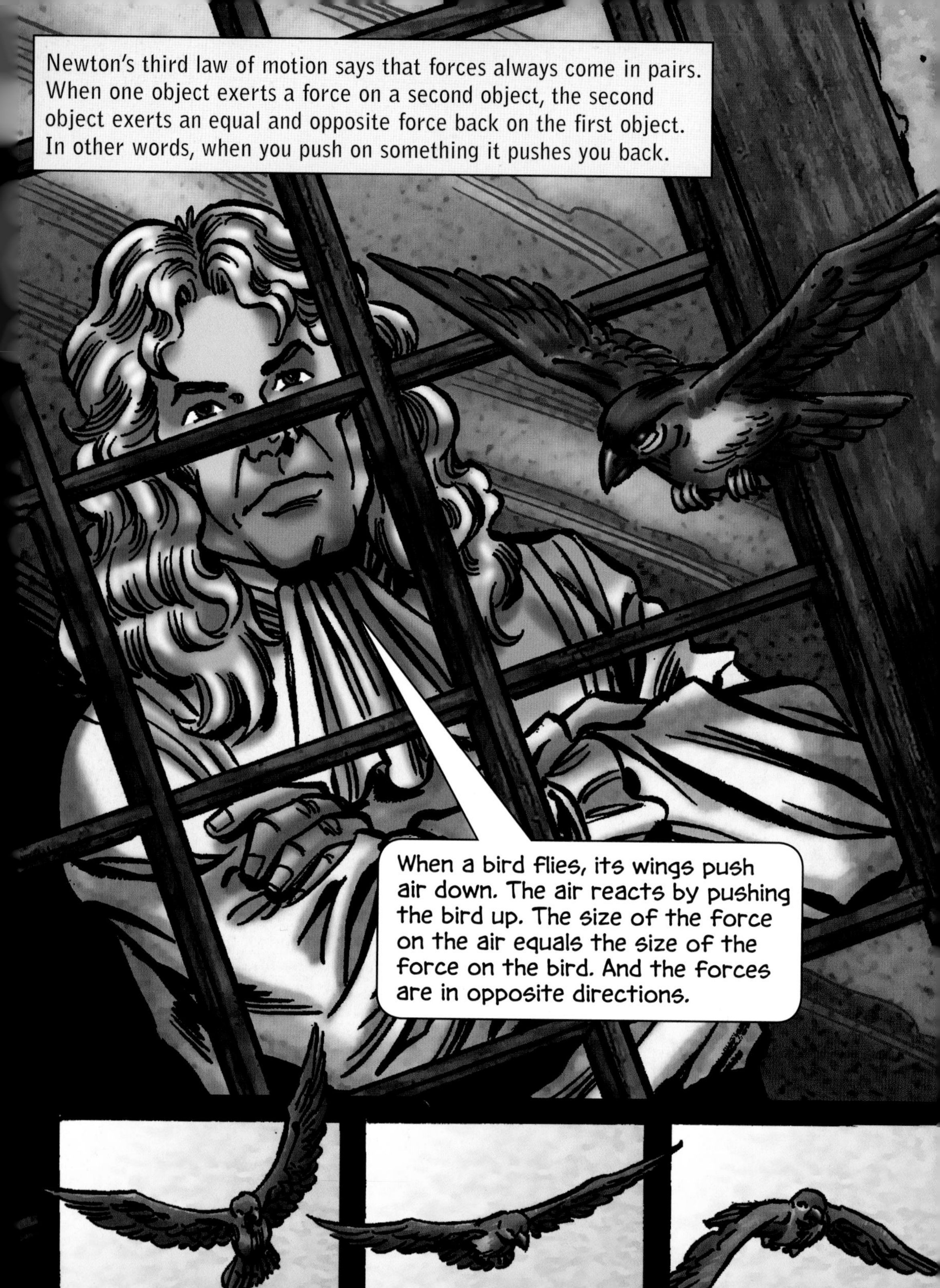
Newton's third law of motion says that forces always come in pairs. When one object exerts a force on a second object, the second object exerts an equal and opposite force back on the first object. In other words, when you push on something it pushes you back.
When a bird flies, its wings push air down. The air reacts by pushing the bird up. The size of the force on the air equals the size of the force on the bird. And the forces are in opposite directions.

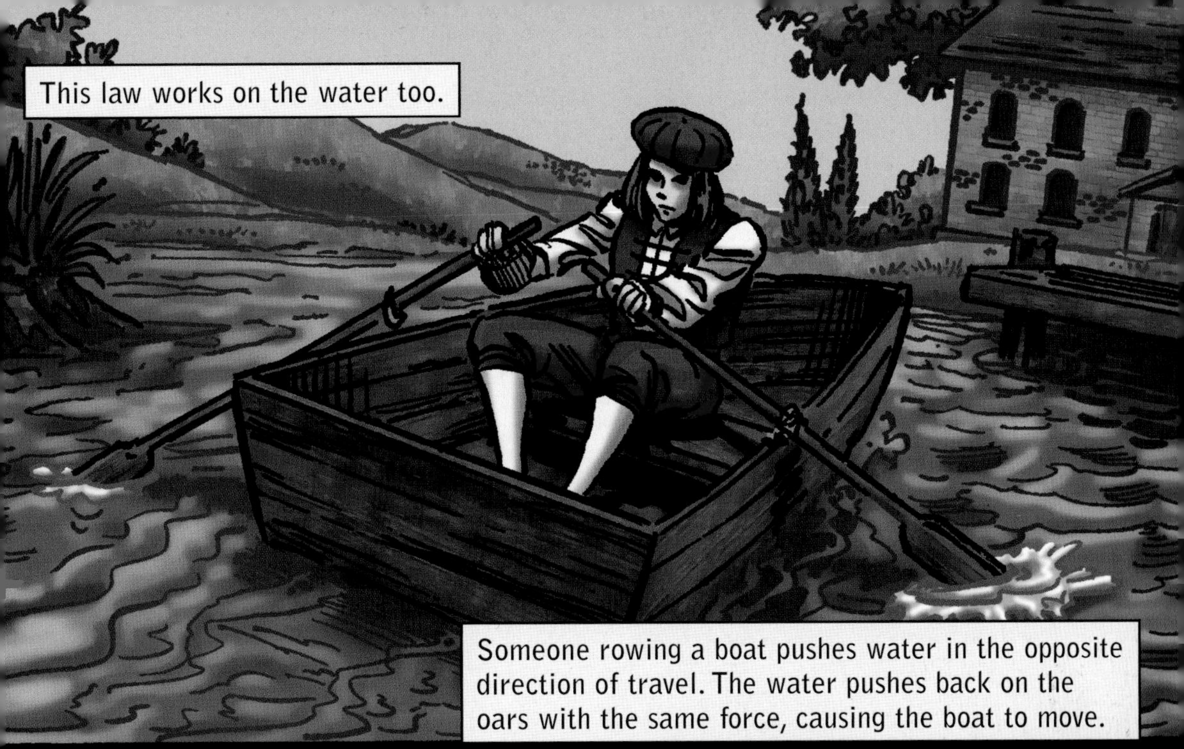

This law works on the water too.
Someone rowing a boat pushes water in the opposite direction of travel. The water pushes back on the oars with the same force, causing the boat to move.

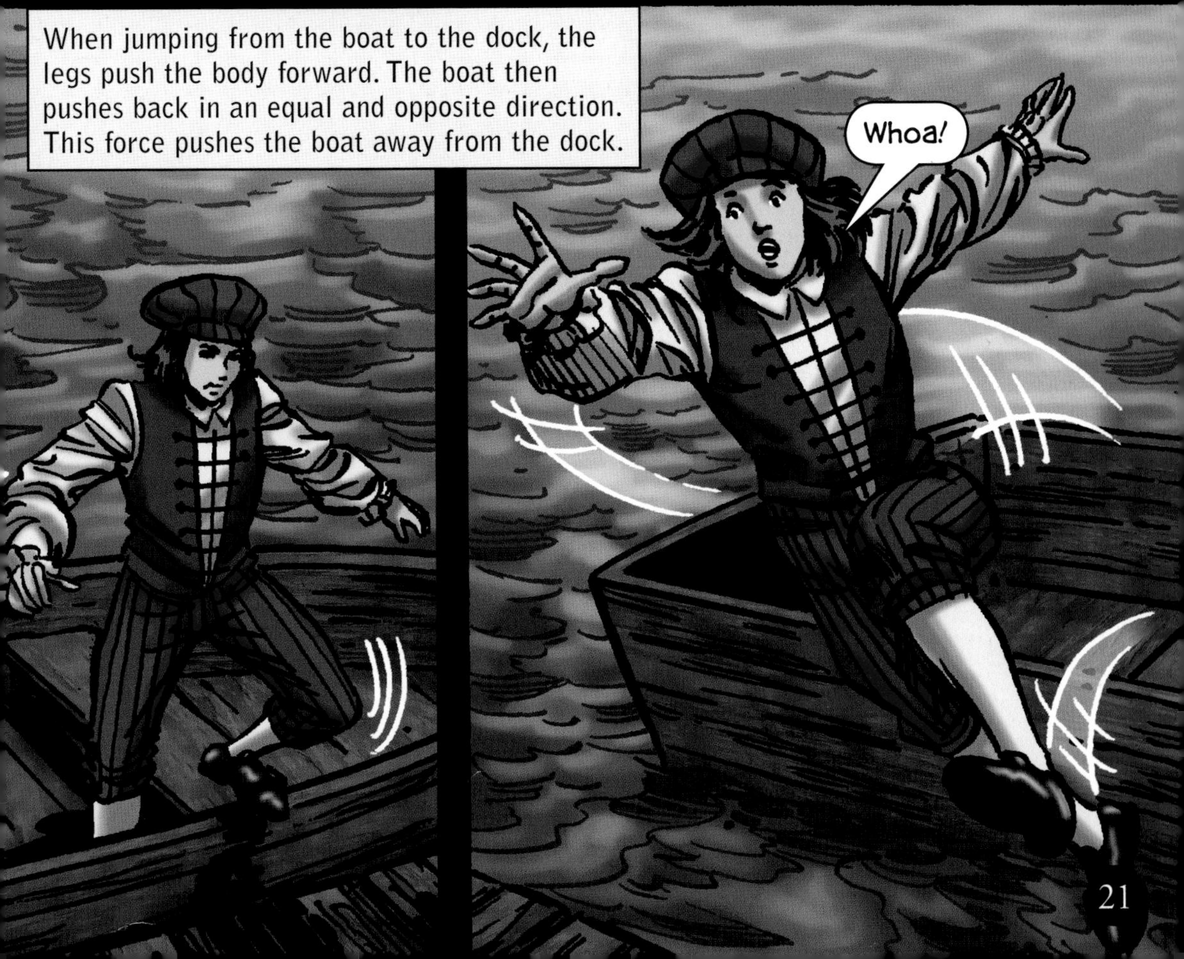

When jumping from the boat to the dock, the legs push the body forward. The boat then pushes back in an equal and opposite direction. This force pushes the boat away from the dock.
Whoa!

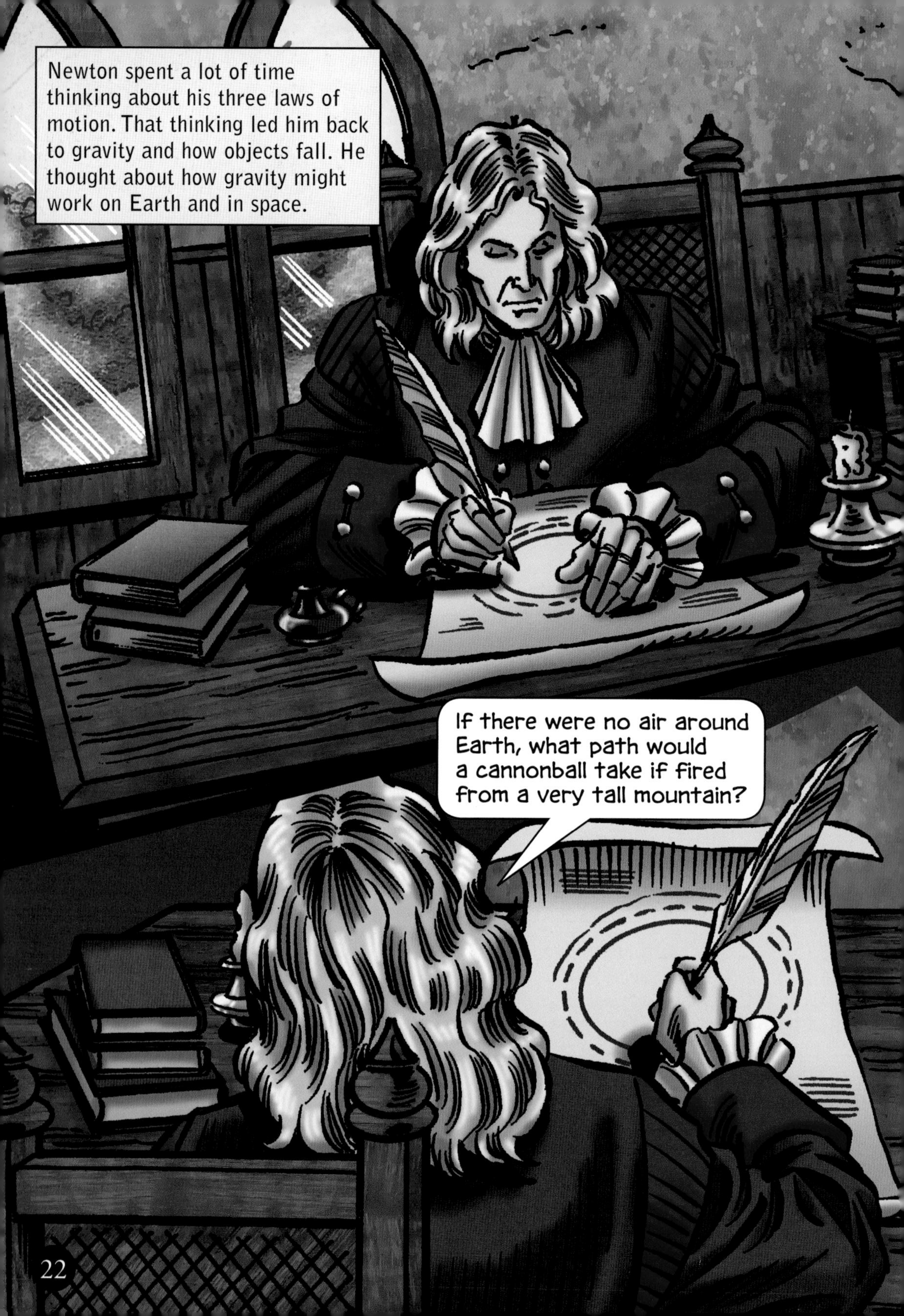
Newton spent a lot of time thinking about his three laws of motion. That thinking led him back to gravity and how objects fall. He thought about how gravity might work on Earth and in space.
If there were no air around Earth, what path would a cannonball take if fired from a very tall mountain?

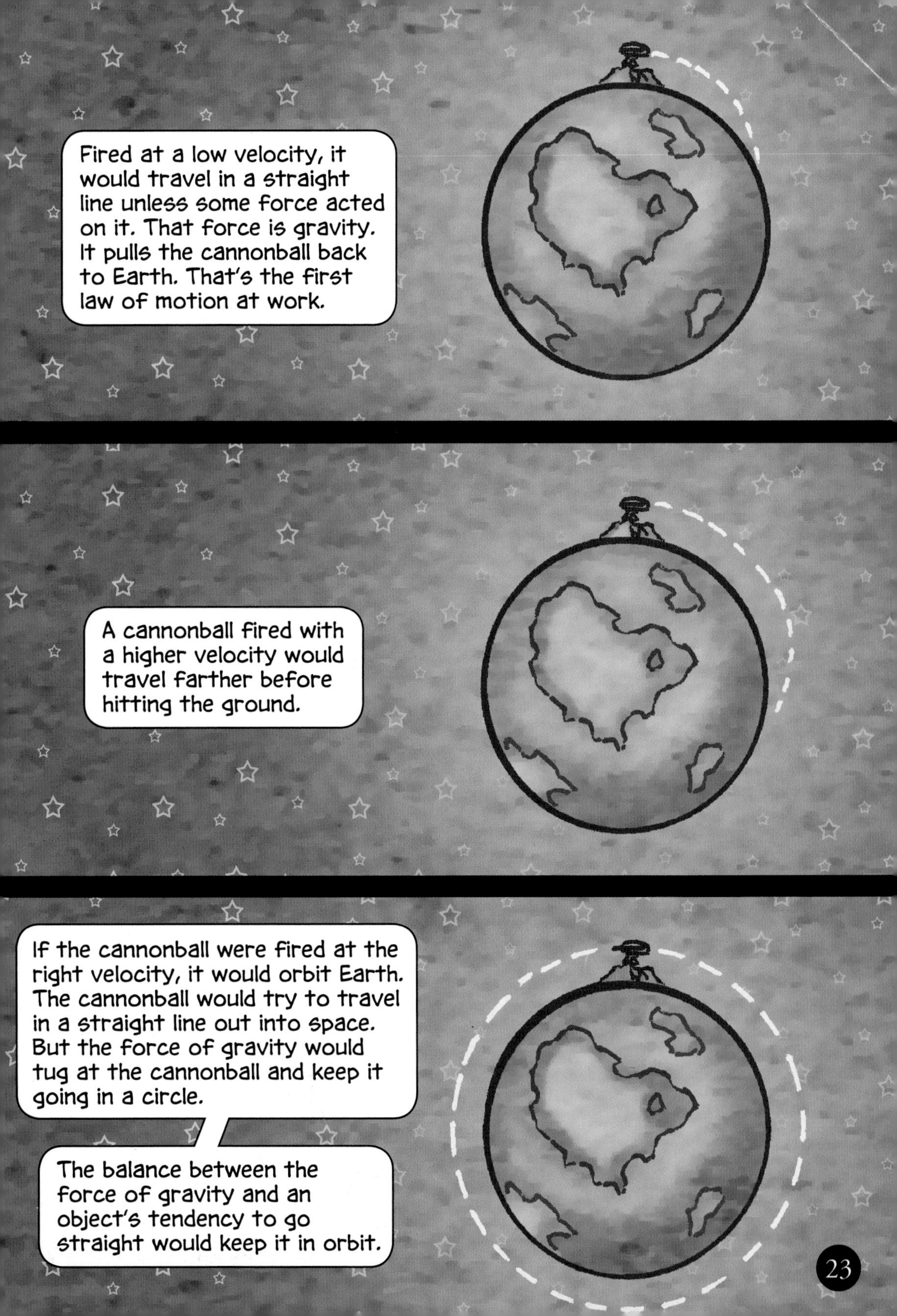

Fired at a low velocity, it would travel in a straight line unless some force acted on it. That force is gravity. It pulls the cannonball back to Earth. That's the first law of motion at work.
A cannonball fired with a higher velocity would travel farther before hitting the ground.
If the cannonball were fired at the right velocity, it would orbit Earth. The cannonball would try to travel in a straight line out into space. But the force of gravity would tug at the cannonball and keep it going in a circle.
The balance between the force of gravity and an object's tendency to go straight would keep it in orbit.

Chapter 4

Newton's Legacy

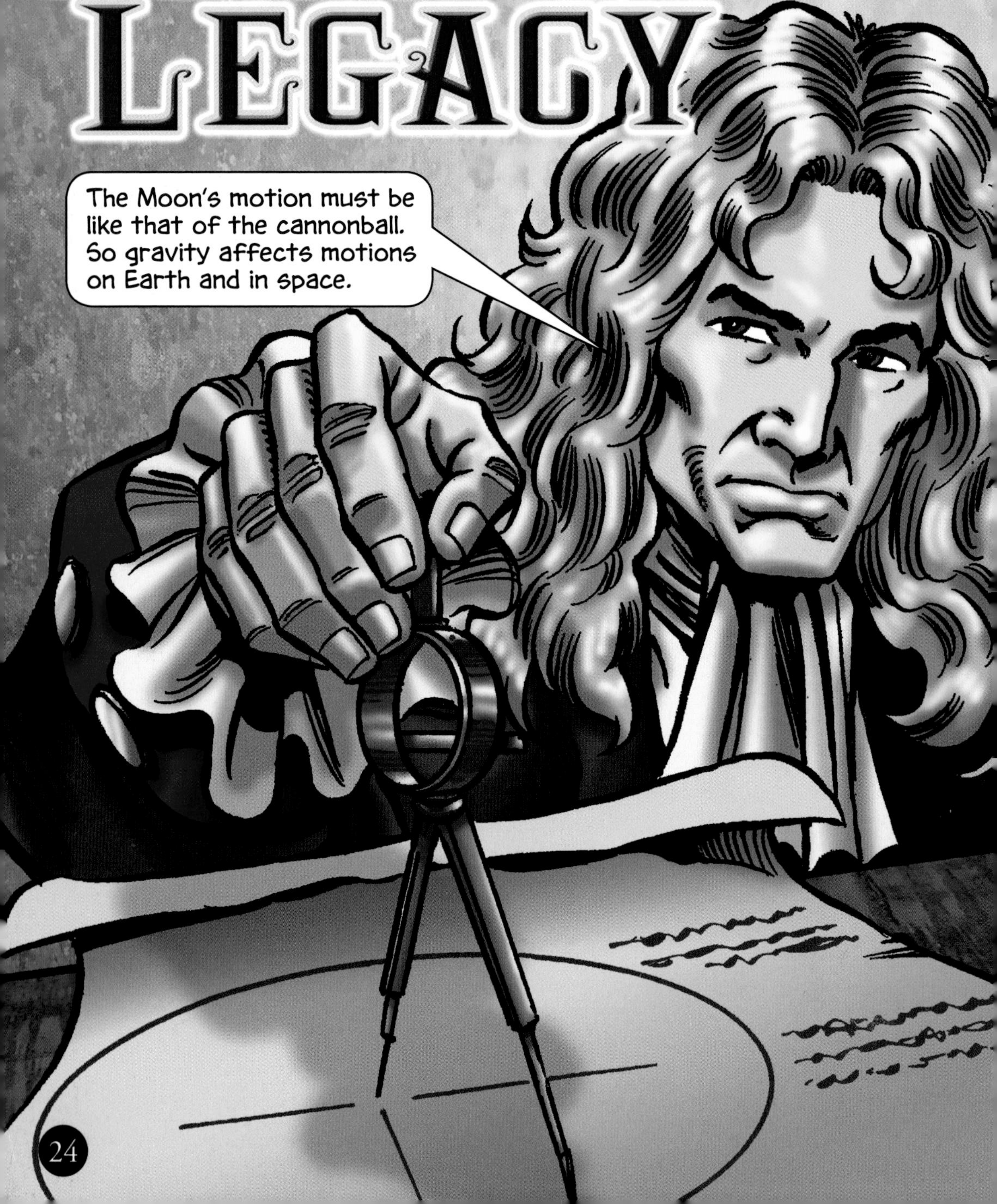
The Moon's motion must be like that of the cannonball. So gravity affects motions on Earth and in space.

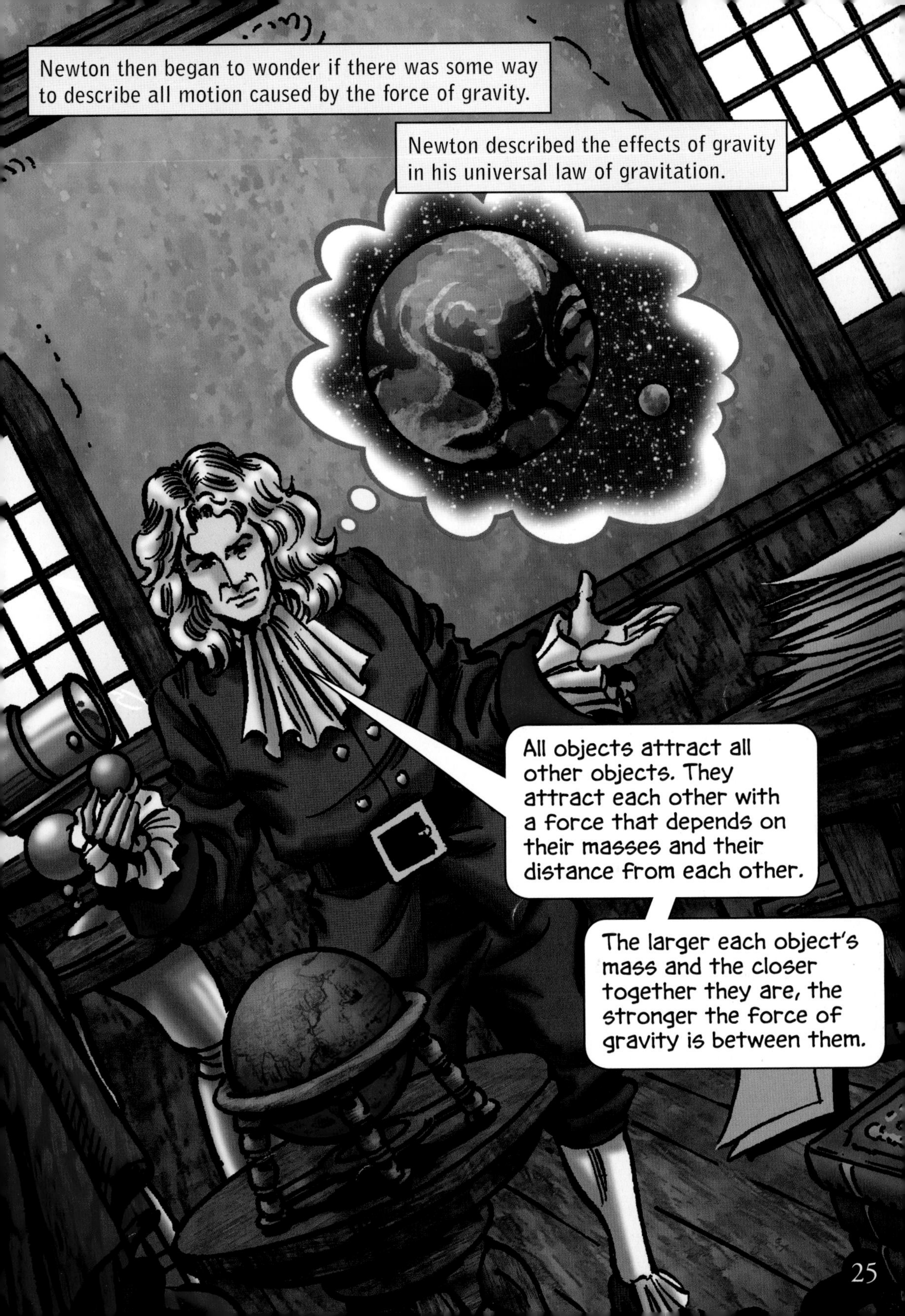
Newton then began to wonder if there was some way to describe all motion caused by the force of gravity.
Newton described the effects of gravity in his universal law of gravitation.
All objects attract all other objects. They attract each other with a force that depends on their masses and their distance from each other.
The larger each object's mass and the closer together they are, the stronger the force of gravity is between them.

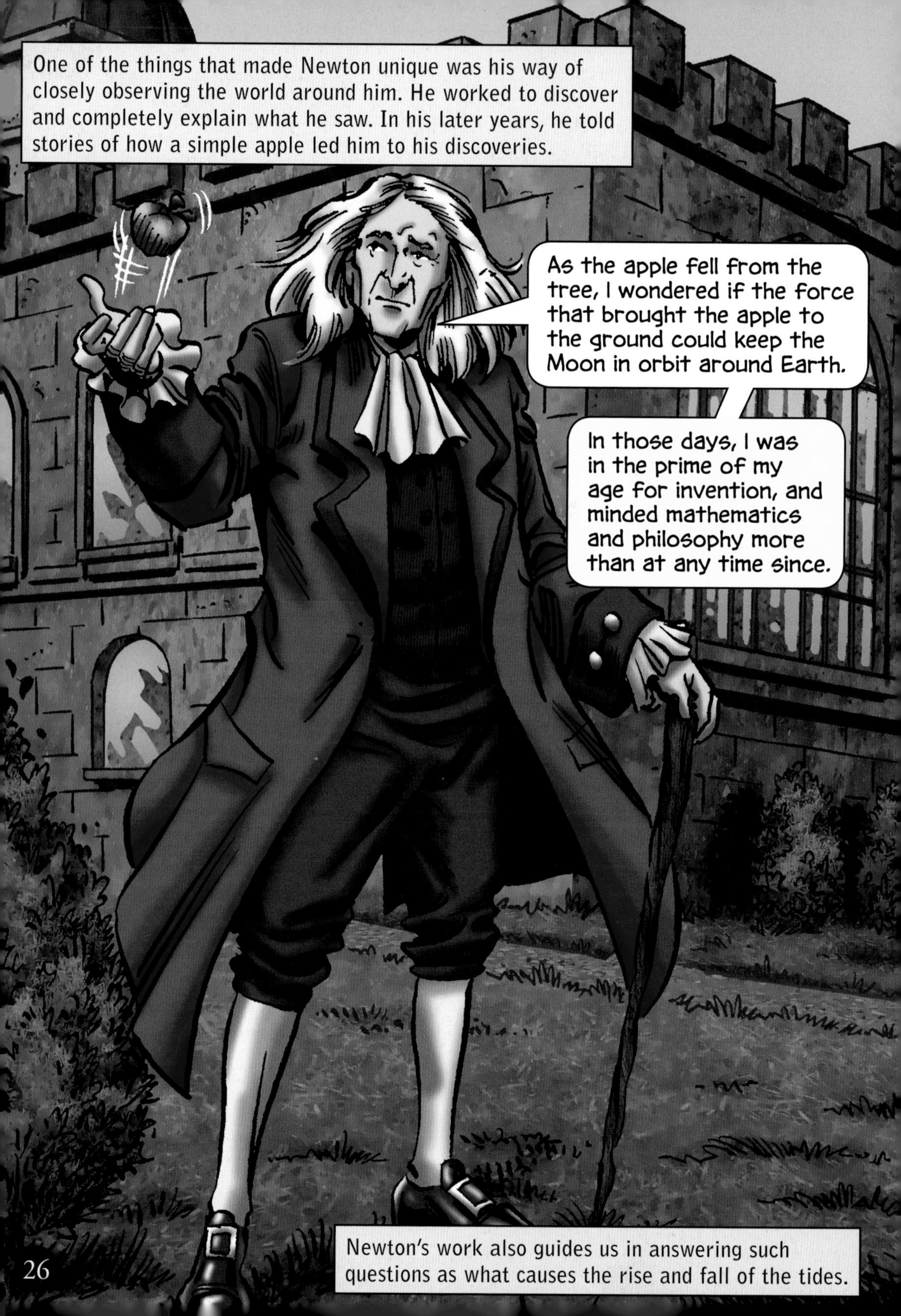
One of the things that made Newton unique was his way of closely observing the world around him. He worked to discover and completely explain what he saw. In his later years, he told stories of how a simple apple led him to his discoveries.
As the apple fell from the tree, I wondered if the force that brought the apple to the ground could keep the Moon in orbit around Earth.
In those days, I was in the prime of my age for invention, and minded mathematics and philosophy more than at any time since.
Newton's work also guides us in answering such questions as what causes the rise and fall of the tides.

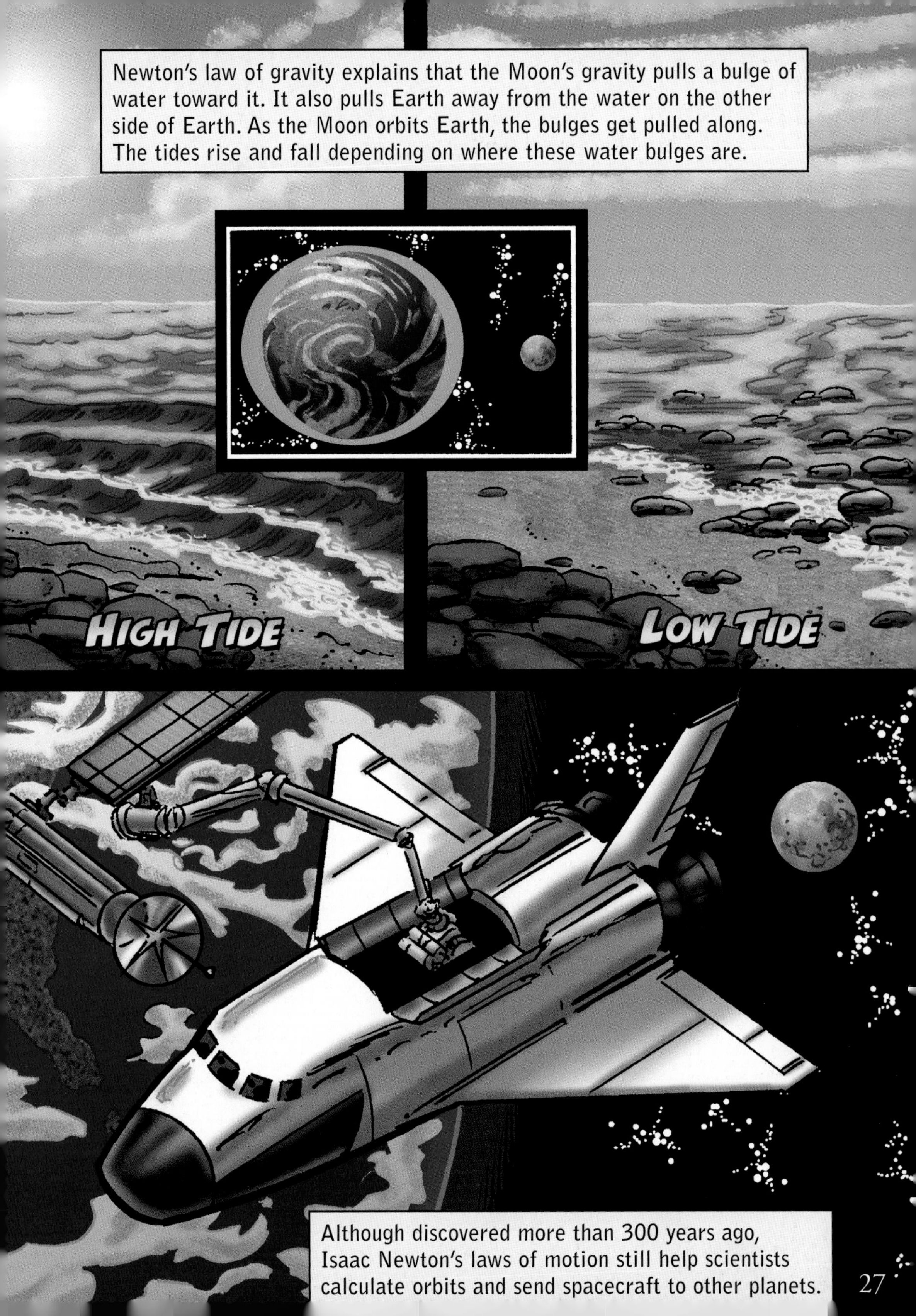
Newton's law of gravity explains that the Moon's gravity pulls a bulge of water toward it. It also pulls Earth away from the water on the other side of Earth. As the Moon orbits Earth, the bulges get pulled along. The tides rise and fall depending on where these water bulges are.
HIGH TIDE
LOW TIDE
Although discovered more than 300 years ago, Isaac Newton's laws of motion still help scientists calculate orbits and send spacecraft to other planets.

ISAAC NEWTON

- **Newton's Laws of Motion:**
  1st Law: An object will stay at rest or in motion in a straight line until some force acts on it.

  2nd Law: The rate of change in velocity of an object depends on the object's mass and on the force acting on that object.

  3rd Law: Forces come in pairs. When one object pushes on another object, that second object pushes back on the first object with a force of the same strength.

- Isaac Newton was born December 25, 1642. He died on March 20, 1727.

- Newton designed and built a new type of telescope. The Newtonian reflecting telescope uses mirrors instead of lenses to bring light from distant objects into focus. Astronomers still use this type of telescope.

- To explain his laws of motion, Newton invented a new kind of math called calculus. Calculus lets you find the length, area, and volume of objects. It also lets you calculate how an object's position and velocity can change with time.

- In 1696, Newton left Trinity College to be Warden of Britain's Royal Mint in London. Newton took his moneymaking duties very seriously. He made the organization much more efficient.

- In 1705, Newton was knighted by Queen Anne. He became known as Sir Isaac Newton. Being knighted is an honor in England given to national heroes.

- Edmond Halley was the astronomer who discovered and predicted the return of a comet. This comet later became known as Halley's comet.

- Newton's discoveries had their roots in the work of many great scientists that came before him. Copernicus, Galileo, and Kepler provided Newton with a foundation on which to build his ideas. Newton once wrote, "If I have seen further than other men, it is because I stood on the shoulders of giants."

- Newton has a scientific measurement named after him. The unit used to measure force is called the newton.

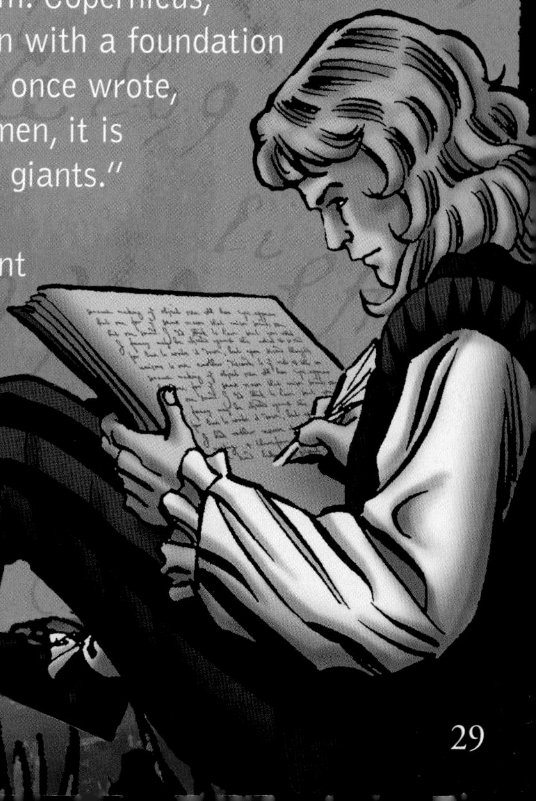

GLOSSARY

equation (e-KWAY-zhuhn)—a mathematical statement, such as 5 x 3 = 15, or 3x + 2 = 14

experiment (ek-SPER-uh-ment)—to test a scientific idea to see its effect

force (FORSS)—any action that changes the movement of an object

gravity (GRAV-uh-tee)—the force that attracts, or pulls, things together

mass (MASS)—the amount of matter an object has

orbit (OR-bit)—the path an object follows as it goes around the Sun or a planet

velocity (vuh-LOSS-uh-tee)—a measurement of both the speed and direction an object is moving

weight (WATE)—the measure of how heavy a person or object is

INTERNET SITES

FactHound offers a safe, fun way to find Internet sites related to this book. All of the sites on FactHound have been researched by our staff.

Here's how:
1. Visit *www.facthound.com*
2. Choose your grade level.
3. Type in this book ID **073686847X** for age-appropriate sites. You may also browse subjects by clicking on letters, or by clicking on pictures and words.
4. Click on the **Fetch It** button.

FactHound will fetch the best sites for you!

READ MORE

Cooper, Christopher. *Forces and Motion: From Push to Shove.* Science Answers. Chicago: Heinemann, 2003.

Halls, Kelly Milner. *Forces and Motion.* Science Fair Projects. Chicago: Heinemann, 2007.

Krull, Kathleen. *Isaac Newton.* Giants of Science. New York: Viking, 2006.

Salas, Laura Purdie. *Discovering Nature's Laws: A Story about Isaac Newton.* A Creative Minds Biography. Minneapolis: Carolrhoda, 2004.

BIBLIOGRAPHY

Hawking, Stephen, ed. *On the Shoulders of Giants: The Great Works of Physics and Astronomy.* Philadelphia: Running Press, 2002.

The Newton Project. http://www.newtonproject.ic.ac.uk/prism.php?id=1

Westfall, Richard S. *Never at Rest: A Biography of Isaac Newton.* Cambridge, England: Cambridge University Press, 1980.

INDEX